AMERICAN
OAK
FURNITURE

STYLES AND PRICES

Other books by Robert W. and Harriett Swedberg

American Clocks and Clockmakers
American Oak Furniture Styles and Prices, Book II, second edition
American Oak Furniture Styles and Prices, Book III, second edition
Antiquing in England: A Guide to Antique Centres
Collectors Encyclopedia of American Furniture, Volume I
Collectors Encyclopedia of American Furniture, Volume II
Country Furniture and Accessories with Prices
Country Furniture and Accessories with Prices, Book II
Country Pine Furniture Styles and Prices, revised edition
Country Store 'N' More
Furniture of the Depression Era
Off Your Rocker
Tins 'N' Bins
Victorian Furniture Styles and Prices, revised edition
Victorian Furniture Styles and Prices, Book II
Victorian Furniture Styles and Prices, Book III
Wicker Furniture Styles and Prices, revised edition

AMERICAN OAK FURNITURE

STYLES AND PRICES

BOOK I

THIRD EDITION

ROBERT W. AND HARRIETT SWEDBERG

Wallace-Homestead Book Company
Radnor, Pennsylvania

Published in Radnor, Pennsylvania 19089, by Wallace-Homestead,
a division of Chilton Book Company

Designed by Anthony Jacobson
Manufactured in the United States of America

Library of Congress Cataloging in Publication Data

Swedberg, Robert W.
    American oak furniture : styles and prices, Book I / Robert W.
Swedberg, Harriett Swedberg.—3rd ed.
      p.   cm.
    Includes bibliographical references (p. 146) and index.
    ISBN 0-87069-621-1 (hc)—ISBN 0-87069-620-3 (pb)
    1. Furniture, Oak—United States—Catalogs.   I. Swedberg,
Harriett.   II. Title.
NK2405.S89   1991b
749.213′075—dc20   91-50432
                                                         CIP

    3 4 5 6 7 8 9 0   10 9 8 7 6 5 4

To
our two beloved daughters,
Cheryl and Karen

Contents

Acknowledgments

The authors are exceedingly grateful to those who generously shared their knowledge and gave of their time to help make this book possible. Most of the shops where photographs were taken offer a general line of merchandise. While they display oak, they do not specialize in this one wood. Our thanks are extended also to those who assisted but did not wish to have their names listed.

Bob Anderson

Antique America
Cheryle, Lance, and Norman Frye
Davenport, Iowa

Antique & Specialty Center
Colleen Higgins and Stephen Bunton
Anchorage, Alaska

Antique Mall
Janet Goetz and Grace Jochimsen
Iowa City, Iowa

The Antique Scene
Lamont and Lillian Hultgren
Moline, Illinois

Antiques at Our House
Richard and Bernice King
Minneapolis, Minnesota

Banowetz Antiques
Virl and Kathy Banowetz
Maquoketa, Iowa

Bill and Dot Best

**Brightview Interiors, Antiques, and
    Collectibles**
Evelyn Maxwell
Milan, Illinois

Denise Brown

Buggy Wheel Antiques
Bill and Gwen Carter
Warsaw, Indiana

Mr. and Mrs. Ralph O. Clark

Country Corners, Ltd.
Jerry and Jeanne Plagge
Latimer, Iowa

Ralph Crafton

Russ and Judy Day

Rev. and Mrs. Kenneth Douglas

Madge Foulk

Four Flags Antique Mall
Niles, Michigan

The Furniture House
Pat and Wynn Scott
Bradford, Illinois

Martha and Wilbur Gibson

Grand River Merchants Antique Mall
George and Gloria VanDusen
Williamston, Michigan

Bob and Mary Grueskin
The Antique Scene
Moline, Illinois

Mr. and Mrs. Byron Hansen

Dee and Bernard Harding

Ron, Nancy, Shane, and Seth Harness

Hillside Antiques
Estelle Holloway
Frankfort, Illinois

Historic House Ltd.
Dale and Teresa Hoffman
Moline, Illinois

The House of Stuff 'N' Things
Ann Figg
Buffalo, Iowa

Carole Hyler

Illinois Antique Center
Dan and Kim Philips
Peoria, Illinois

J. & S. Antiques & Antiques Mall
Jim and Sandy Boender
Manlius, Illinois

Shirley Jessen

Rosemary and Howard Johnson

Kirkham's Korner Antiques
Dolores and Daniel Kirkham
Pierceton, Indiana

LaMere's Furniture Stripping
Leslee and Duane LaMere
Rock Island, Illinois

Rose Lang

Gary and Lorraine Lynch

Mr. and Mrs. James L. Mc Daniel

Melon City Antique Mart
Joe and Mary Cline
Muscatine, Iowa

Miller's Antiques and Collectibles
Bedford, Pennsylvania

Howard Moore

Old Tyme Antiques
Elease Jones
Arcanum, Ohio

Old Village Antiques
Joyce L. Ingram
Williamston, Michigan

Parcel and Harker
East Moline, Illinois

Plainfield Avenue Antique Mall
Larry and Gloria Pratt
Grand Rapids, Michigan

Plaza Antique Mall
Patricia Zwyghuizen
Grand Rapids, Michigan

Pleasant Hill Antique Mall & Tea Room
Bob and Eileen Johnson
East Peoria, Illinois

Prairie Peddler
Terry, Gretchen, and Andy Poffinbarger
Davenport, Iowa

Putnam Street Antiques
Tim Thompson and Gordon Bloomer
Williamston, Michigan

Randy's Antiques
Randy Bahnsen

Robbie's Antiques
Earle and Betty Robison
Lewisburg, Ohio

Anne Ross

Sewing Bird Antiques
Don and Helen Schwenneker
Cordova, Illinois

Introduction

Pricing Oak Furniture

Pricing is difficult, and facts about how prices are set may sound repetitious. But the conclusion is always the same. A price book is merely a guide. Neither the authors nor the publisher assume responsibility for any losses that may be incurred as a result of consulting this guide.

Frequently one overhears that articles at a recent antiques show were priced extremely high. Conversely, people will brag that items at an auction went very low and that they were able to acquire treasures at bargain prices. Who is present and the desirability of a specific article help determine the cost. Perhaps if someone had been competing seriously, the original bidder would have continued fighting upward, encouraged by the talented, cheerleader coaxing of the rapidly chanting auctioneer and the greedy desire he kindles in listeners to take home a prize. Because of this fostered rivalry, people are more apt to exclaim, "You can't buy anything at an auction. Bidders pay even more than they would in shops!"

Participants should decide ahead of time what a fair market value is or how much they can afford to spend and not permit themselves to be chided into exceeding that amount. It is possible for neophytes to bid against themselves, so it is good to become familiar with the action before jumping in. Naturally, items should be inspected for flaws before the singsong pitch commences or the mallet bangs down. While auctions help to establish price trends, they are not a reliable measure of what an object sitting on a store shelf should cost.

There are legitimate questions a dealer may mull over as he puts a price tag on his merchandise. How much was paid for the piece? Would a replacement cost more? What is the current market value? Is the item in good condition? Does it require cleaning, repairing, or refinishing? Has it been altered in any manner—cut down, a new drawer added, the top replaced, a leg repaired? How scarce is it? How old is it? Are there buyers who want it? Is it something with general appeal? Will it sell readily? The concept of supply and demand is ever-changing. An article may be both scarce and old, but if no one wants to give it a home, its price will reflect this. There must be both a buyer and a seller.

PRICE CONSIDERATIONS

Ornateness. Compare the two chairs pictured on page 2. The first, with its turned spindles and pressed design on its top slat (horizontal crosspiece), is the more ornate example. A metal die (mold) was used to press the design of a winged creature into the wood to resemble carving.

Most of the chairs with ornate pressed designs were marketed in the 1890s. By 1910 few were seen in furniture catalogs. By 1915 they were an extinct species.

A later development, popular in the 1920s and 1930s (and seen in the other picture), is referred to currently as a "T-back" because the shape of its back somewhat resembles the letter T. Many people prefer the more decorative chair to the latter, and market prices are re-

Pressed-back chair with solid seat, set of 6. **$275** *each*

Splat-back or T-back chair with leather seat, set of 6. **$90** *each*

Close-up view of winged creature and prey on back of pressed-back chair.

An oak cupboard marriage with a base and top that were not originally together; 43" wide, 18" deep, 85" high. **$775**

A cut-down round oak table that has been made into a lazy Susan with a top that rotates; 42" diameter, 18" high. **$198**

An oak pie safe marriage with added splash back and drawers; 45" wide, 15" deep, 57" to top surface. **$795**

flected by a chair's uniqueness and ornamentation.

Marriage. To an antiquer, a "marriage" refers to the uniting of two unrelated objects to make a new piece. A buyer should be told of a marriage when the seller is aware that one exists. Examine the oak cupboard pictured on page 2.

The base and the top originally were not together. In order to detect a later union, look for variations in style, size, construction details, decorations, or differences in wood patterns, any one of which may indicate that a spurious union has occurred. The pictured pie safe has had a back rail and drawers added to its top that do not match the base. These marriages will lessen values.

Cut-down. It is a popular practice to cut down dining room tables, library tables, or large parlor center tables to coffee-table height. Snacks or drinks of the owner's choice can be served on them as they rest in front of a davenport or chair. The round table pictured has been converted into a lazy Susan with a top that rotates easily. In most cases a cost depreciation occurs in cut-downs.

Uniqueness. When one finds an unusual article, how should it be priced? The dealer-owner of a parlor armchair shown had to decide on a fair price based on the cost of his purchase and the attractiveness of his acquisition.

Another factor in price assignment is, of course, how much profit the owner wishes to make. What value would you place on the oak folding bathtub and combination oak desk washstand (pictured in the color section) if you had been the owner? One dealer facetiously had friends assign a value to a unique game table, a kind she had never seen before, on a piece of paper. The resulting average gave her a price. It is far better, of course, to use research as a basis for determining values on uncommon acquisitions.

Painted or Room Ready. Generally, if a piece of furniture is "room ready," it will sell more easily than one that requires work. A piece needing repair is referred to as being "in the rough." Blemishes, such as burns caused by hot irons or cigarettes, water marks, oil stains, or wood damage may be hidden under a layer of paint. A novice should be wary of purchasing such bargain items, but there is also the existing hope that a real find will be under that paint job.

Availability. The furniture and accessories in this book ordinarily are available to the general public except when items are pictured in private homes. Most of the photographs

Parlor armchair with floral crest on oval back, splayed legs, and H stretchers; 28" arm to arm, 39" high. $225

were taken in the shops mentioned in the Acknowledgments, some of which may no longer be in operation since some of the original photographs that have been retained in this revision date back to 1982. There are no museum photographs included.

CHAPTER 1
Hardy Oak and Its Look-Alikes

It is not surprising that errors frequently are made in the identification of oak because there are five woods—ash, chestnut, elm, hickory, and woods that have been artificially grained to emulate oak—that have similar characteristics.

Ash has a prominent grain that resembles oak. It is heavy, dense, light colored, and strong. Furniture, including frames for upholstered pieces where strength is required, utilize this wood. It bends well for hoops and bow backs on chairs. Its use is generally associated with the twentieth century, when oak became dominant.

However, research shows that it was used in the manufacture of furniture during the latter part of the nineteenth century. In the 1870s, Victorian bedroom sets, for example,

Ash kitchen cupboard with spoon carving and incised lines; 40" wide, 17" deep, 82" high. **$475**

Ash three-quarter-size bed with walnut trim on foot- and headboards; 52" wide, 81" long. **$350**

Ash washstand commode with incised lines and pressed brass backplates and bail handles; 31" wide, 16" deep, 30" high. **$275**

The back of the ash washstand showing the factory marking.

Ash drop-leaf table; 41" by 23", 29" high with 15" drop leaves. **$210**

Ash Eastlake dresser with two decks, swing mirror, applied decorations and candlestands; 37" wide, 17" deep, 76" high. **$575**

were available in both ash and walnut. An ash bed with a 54" high headboard sold for $5.00 through the Nelson, Matter and Co. of Grand Rapids, Michigan, catalog. Its walnut counterpart cost $6.50. A plain washstand ranged from $3.75 in ash to $4.50 in walnut. Ornate styles were priced higher. In 1880 this company offered a three-piece white ash bedroom set with mahogany trim for $100.00. After the turn of the century, ash played an important part in the manufacture of iceboxes. Many of the oak-labeled iceboxes in collectibles and antiques stores today actually were made of ash.

Chestnut is grayish brown and has a coarse, open grain. It is softer, lacks the large rays, and is not as structurally strong as oak, but it resists warping. Before a blight destroyed most of our country's wild chestnut trees in the early 1900s, it was used in furniture manufacturing for the construction of drawers, as a core for veneers, and for use in picture frames and paneling.

Elm is light brown in color, with open pores and an oaklike texture. Because it bends easily and does not readily split, it is suitable for curved parts on furniture, such as hoop backs. Elm has been used largely as a veneer because it has a pleasing pattern and also because of its tendency to warp. Early 1900s catalogs show examples of chairs, iceboxes, and cupboards in elm.

Hickory, a strong, supple wood with an oaklike color and texture, is used for bent parts—especially in the bow backs of chairs, where both thinness and strength are essential.

Oak is light colored, heavy, hard, durable, coarse, and has large open pores. Very distinct pith or medullary rays are exposed when oak is quarter sawed. Elliptical Vs are often seen when it is plain sawed. Oak was popular in this country prior to 1700, but did not become a dominant furniture wood, ex-

Mixed woods (ash, chestnut, and oak) Eastlake marble-top washstand commode with burl veneer drawer panels, chip carving, and incised lines; 28" wide, 16" deep, 40" high. **$550**

Elm kitchen cupboard; 40" wide, 17" deep, 68" high.
$575

Cane-seat-and-back swivel chair with bent parts made of hickory or elm; 20" arm to arm. **$375**

Bent-back kitchen chair with bent parts of hickory or elm; 36" high, set of 4. **$125** *each*

cept for minor revivals, until its rebirth during the 1890 to 1925 period.

Artificial grain is achieved when an inexpensive wood with little or no pattern is stroked with a color and wood figure that resembles oak. Special rollers, combs, brushes, rags, sponges, and crumpled paper are used to artificially grain wood. Small hotels and families of modest means purchased the less-costly furniture so they could have what appeared to be up-to-date oak furnishings.

You can often detect this type of graining by inspecting the inside of the solid wood (not veneered) drawer fronts to note whether the pattern has similar characteristics on both sides. On a stand or table, the underside of the top can be inspected for the same purpose. Often, because of age and wear on drawer and door fronts around the handles or on the top, some of the graining may have worn away, exposing an unpatterned subsurface. Be aware, too, that paint remover will flush the grain down the drain.

*Plain-sawed oak parlor table showing elliptical Vs; 23"
by 24", 30" high.* **$125**

*Artificial-oak-grained dresser to resemble quarter-sawed
oak; 44" wide, 23" deep, 76" high.* **$245**

*Quarter-sawed oak chiffonier with serpentine drawer
fronts; 34" wide, 19" deep, 48" high;* **$395.** *Japanese
octagonal school wall clock,* **$225;** *Ingraham shelf clock,*
$165.

Popular oak finishes emerged in the late
1800s when David W. Kendall, one of Grand
Rapids, Michigan's, first furniture designers,
observed that workers who chewed tobacco
spit the juice on the oak floors in the factories.
In time this had a tendency to darken the
floorboards. Because the resulting color ap-
pealed to Kendall, he attempted to achieve
the same effect by rubbing tobacco liquid on
furniture, but the resulting nicotine stain was

Quarter-sawed oak S-curved rolltop desk; 55" wide, 36" deep, 46" high. **$3,800**

Quarter-sawed oak child's rocker with rolled seat and veneered back; 15" arm to arm, 24" high. **$143**

Quarter-sawed and plain-sawed oak Roman chair with medallions, head carvings, and paw feet; 25" arm to arm, 38" high. **$325**

Buffet base from which veneer and artificial graining have been stripped except for the open door on the right that retains its quarter-sawed oak appearance; 46" wide, 21" deep, 36" high. **$125**

not permanent. When he achieved a similar color with the use of chemicals, competitors laughed and dubbed his successful dark finish "mud." However, when Kendall's antique oak products became a marketable commodity, his one-time deriders hastened to copy his color.

Other early 1900 choices of finish, in-cluding the popular fumed oak, were available. The 1908 Sears catalog offered a new cupboard design in "hardwood with solid oak front, high gloss golden finish." Elm iceboxes received similar treatment, as did hotel commode washstands made of northern hardwoods.

CHAPTER 2

The Entry Hall

What furniture is helpful to family members and guests alike when they enter a home? One such piece was a *hall tree,* a place where hats, coats, umbrellas, and even overshoes could be kept temporarily.

Another storage unit available in the late 1800s and early 1900s was *a lift-lid bench* that provided a seat where overshoes could be removed and a place for storage.

Customarily, a *matching mirror* hung on the wall above the bench and had hat and coat hooks to accommodate outdoor clothing. Originally benches and mirrors could be purchased individually or as a set. In the course of time, however, some of these sets became separated. Since the mirror was less bulky and could be used more easily in a home's decor, it is more prevalent in today's antiques market than the benches.

A hall tree is an all-inclusive unit that

Lift-lid hall bench and accompanying beveled mirror with 4 double hooks: bench, 39" wide, 17" deep, 38" high; mirror, 36" wide, 24" high. **$795**

Lift-lid hall bench and accompanying mirror with 4 double hooks and applied decorations: Bench is 52" wide, 19" deep, 38" high. Mirror is 53" wide, 27" deep. **$2,495**

usually provides hooks for hanging outer garments and a place to put folded and wet umbrellas. The excess water from the umbrellas is caught by metal drip pans. At times a lift-lid bench served as a storage and sitting site. Values of hall trees are determined largely by the construction, decorations and hand carving, kinds of hooks, beveled mirror, paw feet, and other features that elevate a piece from the plain to fancy classification.

Originally a *pier mirror,* which often featured a narrow shelf near the base, stood tall in its own special place between two long windows. Later these mirrors found their way into the entry hall in many homes.

A gracious, interesting entranceway serves another purpose. It invites guests to "come on in," as the choice items from the past situated there welcome the visitors.

Hall tree with lift-lid bench, 4 double hat hooks and applied decorations; 25" wide, 16" deep, 80" high. **$590**

Hall tree with lift-lid bench, 4 double hat hooks and applied decorations; 30" arm to arm, 16" deep, 80" high. **$1,295**

Hall tree with lift-lid bench, 4 double hat hooks and applied decorations; 31" arm to arm, 16" deep, 82" high. **$575**

Pier mirror with applied decorations and carvings; 26" wide, 88" high with 8" shelf depth. **$1,095**

Cherry and oak lift-lid hall bench with applied decorations; 36" wide, 20" deep, 39" high. **$425**

Hall mirror with 4 double hat hooks; 23" wide, 33" high. **$225**

Mirror with 2 double hat hooks, beveled mirror, and applied decorations; 36" wide, 72" high. **$395**

Hat and umbrella rack with tin drip pan and 2 replaced brass hat hooks; 15" wide, 14" deep, 68" high. **$185**

Hall mirror with 4 double hat hooks, beveled mirror, and applied decorations; 23" wide, 32" high. **$145**

Hall mirror with 4 double hat hooks; 34" wide, 22" high. **$225**

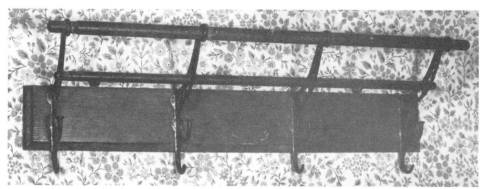

School coat and hat rack with a label that reads "Odell's Hat and Coat Rack, pat. Nov. 1, '87 mfg. by the Odell Iron Works, Indianapolis"; 24" wide, 7" deep. **$145**

Hall mirror with three double hat hooks and applied beading; 18" square. **$250**

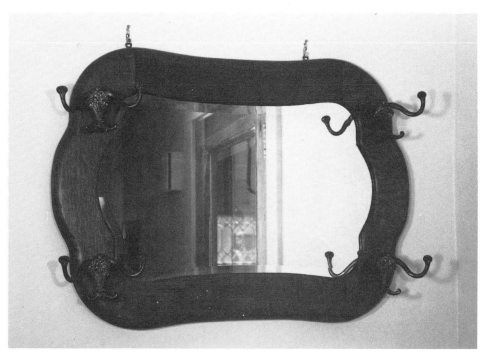

Hall mirror with 4 double hat hooks; 33" wide, 22" high. **$225**

Hall mirror with 4 double hat hooks and applied edge beading; 30" wide, 20" high. **$195**

Hall mirror with 4 copper-washed hat hooks; 30" wide, 21" high. **$175**

CHAPTER 3
The Living Room

In the 1800s the parlor was a reserved room. Special guests—such as the parson or priest, visiting friends, the daughter's beau or business acquaintances—were entertained there. It was set apart for these special people and was not a place where the family gathered. Editorials in women's magazines at the turn of the century deplored this tradition. They believed that the residents of the home were more important than guests who came and went. Because of this widely generated feeling, the family oriented living room was born, even though the term parlor also remained in use. While each house is unique in its decor, some pieces are commonly associated with the living room.

Although seats of all sorts are of paramount importance in a living room, various kinds are found in almost every room of the house. Straight chairs and benches are pictured and discussed in Chapter 5, whereas examples of mission seating can be found in the color section and Chapter 10. Children's sizes and office kinds are found in the chapters dealing with those types of furniture.

Rocking chairs generally are popular with Americans, who like the gentle, swaying motion. On the contrary, some Europeans are

Platform rocker with applied beading and decorations; 23" arm to arm, 38" high. **$315**

Platform rocker with pressed top rail and slat; 23" arm to arm, 42" high. **$300**

apprehensive and fear they will fall over backwards. Chairs occasionally "creep" to the edge of a porch and fall off, causing injury to the occupant. Rockers also tend to wear out rugs, much to the distress of some housewives. Various patented chairs, called "patent" or "platform" rockers, which swayed on attached foundations or platforms, were developed to counteract these problems. Occasionally a patent date can be found on the metal parts in the base. A multitude of other types of rockers were built with and without arms; with upholstered, cane, wooden, and rush seats; with pressed, splat, slat, and spindled backs; and those serving special services or functions, such as sewing or slipper rockers.

Shaker ladder-back rocker with woven seat; 22" arm to arm, 42" high. **$400**

Rocker with upholstered seat and back; 26" arm to arm, 41" high. **$150**

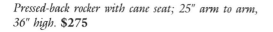

Pressed-back rocker with cane seat; 25" arm to arm, 36" high. **$275**

Armchair rocker; 25" arm to arm, 40" high. **$200**

Quadruple-pressed-back rocker with cane seat; 38" high. **$125**

Pressed-back rocker with Man of the North Wind design; 39" high. **$200**

Spindle-back rocker with splint seat; 39" high. **$215**

Rocker with leather seat and spindled back; 42" high.
$225

Sewing rocker with cane seat and spindled back; 35" high. **$65**

Upholstered furniture was abundant and versatile. A modern term used to describe a couch with a built-in pillow at one end is a "fainting couch." This term has not been found in any of the twentieth-century furniture catalogs that the authors examined. Upholstered couches with arms that folded down to provide a sleeping space were prevalent. Some

Divan or loveseat with floral crest; 36" wide, 20" deep, 39" high. **$375**

Loveseat with incised carving; 38" arm to arm, 23" deep, 34" high. **$495**

Combination desk-washstand made by Windsor Folding Bed, patented June 9, 1885; 31" wide, 27" deep at base, 66" high. **$1,325**

Built-in buffet, photographed in a 1913 Arts and Crafts bungalow in Iowa, with flanking china cupboards and leaded glass doors; 139" wide, 57" high.

Extension dining room table from the early 1900s with pedestal base, twisted Jacobean-type legs and six leaves; 55" square, 30" high. Six chairs that originally had caned center backs; 43" high. Seven-piece set is $1,750. Tea cart near windows; 33" wide, 18" deep, 27" high. $295

"Quaint Furniture," Stickley Bros. Co. desk; 36" wide, 23" deep, 36" high. A two-piece set with matching armchair that is not shown is **$900.**

"Quaint Furniture," Stickley Bros. Co., Grand Rapids, Michigan, original finish round lamp table with leg tenons through the top; 24" diameter, 30" high; $650. Table lamp with copper and slag glass shade; 18" square, 24" high; $800. L. and J. G. Stickley quarter-sawed oak slatted armchair with pegs, through-arm tenons and a beveled front seat rail (an L. and J. G. Stickley design); 28" arm to arm, 26" deep, 38" high; $800. The pieces on the back shelves are examples of Arts and Crafts candlesticks and pottery by Roseville, Weller, VanBriggle, McCoy, Teco, Fulper, and Marblehead.

"Quaint Furniture," Stickley Bros. Co. settle that can be found in one of their catalogs; 62" wide, 26" deep, 37" high. **$950**

Seen from left to right: A J. M. Young, New York, quarter-sawed oak Morris-type chair featuring side slats to the base stretcher, corbels on arms, through- or exposed arm tenons, and a wooden bar at the back to adjust reclining position; 31" arm to arm, 37" deep, 36" high; **$1,200.** *Quarter-sawed round oak lamp table, possibly handcrafted as it hasn't been found in catalogs; 24" diameter, 28" high;* **$350.** *Mission-style wooden table lamp with a slag glass shade; 16" square, 23" high;* **$295.** *Unknown maker mission rocker with slats under arms, front arm corbels and exposed arm tenons; 32" arm to arm, 29" deep, 36" high;* **$800.**

Imperial Furniture Co., Grand Rapids, Michigan, quarter-sawed oak library table with applied tenons on legs and side stretchers, slatted sides, and triangular-shaped copper drawer pulls; 50" wide, 32" deep, 30" high. **$450**

L. and J. G. Stickley quarter-sawed oak sideboard with plate rail, pegged construction, and hand-hammered copper escutcheon plates and drawer pulls; 48" wide, 20" deep, 36" high, 8" plate rail, **$1,200.**

L. and J. G. Stickley quarter-sawed oak highboy dresser with pegged construction and hand-hammered copper drawer pulls; 40" wide, 21" deep, 47" high; **$1,650;** with attached swing mirror, **$2,500.**

Harden quarter-sawed oak mission rocker with curved arms, long side slats, through tenons on front of box, and through-arm tenons; 30" arm to arm, 36" high. **$700**

Gustav Stickley library table with corbels on legs, pegged construction, through-leg tenons and hammered copper drawer pulls. **$650**

Sofa that converts into a double bed with black tufted leatherlike upholstery, scrolled arms and legs, serpentine base and claw feet; 83" arm to arm, 36" deep, 44" high. **$2,995**

China cabinet with two convex glass side panels, two convex glass door panels, and a front center door with designs on the glass; 46" wide, 17" deep, 77" high. $1,450

Roycroft chair with an impressed cross and orb trademark symbol (for a close-up of this symbol see Chapter 10) in the center of the front apron; 40" high. $450

Quarter-sawed oak mission china cabinet with muntins on doors and side panels; 38" wide, 16" deep, 57" high; $650. The wooden mission table lamp on the top of the cabinet has a slag shade; 14" square, 21" high; $350.

Copper-lined folding bathtub with a copper water reservoir; 27" wide, 65" in length, 73" high. **$3,250**

featured a pullout section that doubled the reclining area. One handy type provided a storage area for bedding. Sofas that could be converted into beds were developed, and an example is pictured in the color section.

Settee with incised carving; 46" arm to arm, 22" deep, 40" high. **$595**

Couch, circa 1889, with arms that fold down; 55" arm to arm, 31" deep, 34" high. **$495**

Couch with upholstered seat, sides, and back, and side arms that lower for conversion into a bed; 59" wide, 28" deep, 39" high. **$298**

Parlor suites were sold with various combinations of pieces. A dainty matching divan, armchair, and parlor chair comprised a three-piece set. By adding a rocker, sofa, and a few more parlor chairs, a ten-piece set resulted.

Library tables, often rectangular or oval, were repositories of newspapers and magazines. A drawer was usually present in the front apron, and occasionally one went through on both sides, enabling the user to work from either side. When included, bookshelves were handy additions.

Oval library table with handleless drawer and pillar legs; 38" wide, 24" deep, 30" high. **$345**

Library table with twisted and spool-turned legs; 34" wide, 22" deep, 28" high. **$225**

Library table with curved apron, lyre-type legs and paw feet; 45" wide, 26" deep, 30" high. **$575**

Library table with lyre-type legs; 42" wide, 26" deep, 29" high. **$325**

Library table with cabriole legs; 29" wide, 22" deep, 29" high. **$225**

Library table with grooved legs; 32" wide, 23" deep, 30" high. **$395**

Plant stands varied in height from the short taboret (tabouret) type to tall stands that frequently held a fern, whose leaves fell gracefully down the sides of the stand.

Lamp tables were abundant because many homes were not electrified in the early part of the 1900s, and they provided a place for kerosene lamps or, in some instances, candles. Also available were lamps that could be converted to electricity.

Taboret or plant stand with scalloped top; 12" square, 15" high. **$125**

*Taboret or plant stand with keyhole design in legs; 12"
square, 19" high.* **$100**

*Plant stand with splayed legs and base shelf; 16" square,
31" high.* **$85**

*Taboret or plant stand with hexagonal top and ball
and stick design between legs; 14" square, 21" high.*
$165

Plant stand with hexagonal top; 14" square, 20" high.
$95

Parlor tables commonly had oval, square, rectangular, and cloverleaf tops, and many came with base shelves. To add uniqueness leg shapes varied from cabriole, reeded, fluted, to straight types, some of which terminated with paw or claw feet. Applied decorations and carving, real carving, and incised lines and designs gave each table individuality. Sometimes floral or animal motifs were added to promote salability.

Parlor table with scalloped top, base shelf, and turned legs; 30" wide, 22" deep, 29" high. **$150**

Parlor table with beading on base shelf and apron, twisted legs, and one-piece brass ball and claw feet; 30" square, 30" high. **$495**

Parlor table with cut-out provision in top and lower shelf for chair; 26" wide, 20" deep, 29" high. **$250**

Parlor table with octagonal top, scalloped base shelf, and twisted legs; 26" wide, 29" high. **$300**

Parlor table with applied decorations, incised designs, and reeded legs; 28" square, 30" high. **$395**

Parlor table with beading and ball and claw feet; 24" square, 30" high. **$150**

Parlor table with scalloped top, twist-turned legs, and shelf that is attached to the legs with metal brackets; 23" square, 29" high. **$185**

Parlor table with serpentine apron, scalloped top, and base shelf; 24" square, 30" high. **$345**

Worktable with carved designs on two doors; 41" wide, 20" deep, 32" high. **$375**

Research in the Grand Rapids Public Library in Grand Rapids, Michigan, reveals that this city was America's furniture capital in the last half of the 1800s. During the twenty-year period from 1880 to 1900, more that eighty-five furniture manufacturers started in business there, including Stickley Brothers Company. There the brothers worked together and created the furniture typical of that time. Gustav and a partner, and later Leopold joined by J. George established their own factories in New York State. Albert became president of Stickley Brothers Company. A pictured folding parlor table with spool-type legs is marked "Quaint Furniture, Stickley Bros. Co., Grand Rapids, Mich." It does not feature the lines typical of mission-style furniture that one usually associates with the Quaint label.

Each reader can conjure up a different picture of an oak-filled parlor of the early 1900s, but in the main, all of the kinds of furniture that were found there are pictured in this chapter and Chapter 5 (which deals with chairs and benches) and Chapter 10 (which shows mission furniture pieces, some of which may be found in the living room).

Oval folding parlor table with spool legs and a label underneath reading, "Quaint Furniture, Stickley Bros. Co., Grand Rapids, Mich."; 24" wide, 19" deep, 24" high. **$400**

Game table, late 1880s, with cabriole legs and concave bottom shelf that allows for leg room. The removed top shows spinning pointers for a game; 32" square, 29" high. **$650**

Liquor cabinet with scroll feet and a door with shelves for holding bottles; 20" wide, 16" deep, 34" high. **$175**

Whatnot stand with artificially grained shelf supports and ladder-back to imitate bamboo; 16" wide, 12" deep, 37" high. **$175**

The label found underneath the oval folding table.

CHAPTER 4
The Dining Room

In the late 1800s, and as a new century began, large oak *extension tables* provided space for Sunday family dinners, often with married siblings and their children joining Grandma and Grandpa for the afterchurch meal.

When neighboring farmers cooperatively formed work crews, they all labored together in sequence at one another's farms to help thresh the wheat, oats, or similar crops. The host family, with the help of the other farmer's wives and older daughters, prepared and served a huge meal to all of the workers. A large, expandable table was necessary to fit all of the food and hungry workers.

In 1897 Sears offered a round *drop-leaf table* with five legs; the central leg served to support added leaves. The six-foot size sold for $3.40 while a ten-foot table cost $5.00. This was the only style of round table advertised. No pillar (pedestal) tables were illustrated, either. The six other tables pictured were square, and an ash example was the least expensive.

Square extension table with six bulbous reeded legs and concave stretchers with ball decorations; 44" square, 29" high. **$875**

Round pedestal extension table; 54" diameter, 30" hiah. **$950**

The 54" diameter table with the pedestal divided.

*Square extension table with center support leg; 42"
square, 31" high.* **$415**

*Square extension table with five reeded legs; 42" square,
30" high.* **$425**

*Square extension table with center support leg, paw
feet, and six leaves; 44" square, 30" high.* **$1,050**

*Queen Anne extension table with two center legs that
remain stationary when the leaves are added, made by
"Spencer Table and Chair Co., Marion, Ind."; 45"
by 55", 30" high.* **$500**

This $5.28 ash version extended to twelve
feet. The finest, most expensive oak example
in the twelve-foot size sold for $17.50. Fancy
brackets connected the two legs at each end,
and the middle leg was free to move in support of additional leaves.

Train freight was an added cost. Generally tables were sent "knocked down" and were
put together by the buyer, who followed the
clear-cut assembly directions. In small towns,
those who did not use mail-order catalog service could purchase merchandise in the furniture store, which often was owned and operated by the local funeral director.

Round pillar tables, advertised as such in
early catalogs of the twentieth century, now
are called pedestal tables.

In 1902 Sears pictured not only "the old-
fashioned round drop-leaf table" that extended, but also solid oak round pillar tables
as well. The plainest in the twelve-foot expanded size sold for $11.60. The most elab-
orate example was made of quarter-sawed oak
with a beaded molding on the apron. The legs
that extended from the center pillar were carved
and ornamented and had paw feet. A full range

Double pedestal extension table with veneered apron and pedestals; 42" square, 30" high. **$795**

Round pedestal extension table with beading on apron and paw feet; 45" diameter, 30" high. **$975**

Round pedestal extension table that has two auxiliary supporting legs that drop down on each side when the table is opened, and scroll feet; 48" diameter, 29" high. **$575**

Round extension table with double pedestal base and paw feet; 45" diameter, 30" high. **$1,300**

Pedestal base for extension table with lion heads and paw feet. Complete table is **$1,950.**

Sideboard with applied decorations and grotesque near the top; 48" wide, 24" deep, 77" high. **$1,895**

Round pedestal extension table with paw feet; 45" diameter, 29" high. **$925**

of square-topped oak extension tables, all with five legs, were available.

Currently dealers prefer the round extension tables because they outsell the square varieties. Usually, extra leaves have to be stored away when not in use, but in some cases, tables are constructed so that the leaves are self-storing and can be slid into place as needed.

Sideboards or buffets serve as storage units for articles such as glass, china, silverware, and linens that will be used on the table. In this book the term "sideboard" is used for the more elaborate, ostentatious version and "buffet" for the humbler variety, although each fulfills the same function.

Sideboard with applied decorations and pillars supporting top shelf; 48" wide, 23" deep, 76" high. **$995**

Sideboard with applied decorations, serpentine drawers, and paw feet; 45" wide, 21" deep, 79" high. **$850**

Sideboard with applied decorations and pillars supporting top shelf; 41" wide, 20" deep, 78" high. **$695**

Sideboard with applied decorations; 40" wide, 19" deep, 74" high. **$595**

Sideboard with applied decorations on bottom doors and serpentine-projection top drawers; 42" wide, 20" deep, 63" high. **$825**

Sideboard with applied decorations, serpentine drawers, and shelves supported by scrolled pillars; 45" wide, 21" deep, 75" high. **$695**

Sideboard with applied decorations on bottom doors; 46" wide, 23" deep, 65" high. **$625**

Buffet with swell-projection top drawers, scroll feet, and mirror supports, a style called "colonial" in the catalogs of the 1920s; 54" wide, 23" deep, 54" high. **$425**

Mission-style oak buffet; 55" wide, 18" deep, 51" high. **$395**

Sideboard with applied decorations and projection drawers; 44" wide, 22" deep, 77" high. **$625**

Buffet or server with cabriole legs; 38" wide, 18" deep, 46" high. **$425**

Buffet with scroll feet and candle brackets flanking mirror; 40" wide, 20" deep, 59" high. **$485**

Buffet with applied decorations and open storage space near base; 45" wide, 21" deep, 58" high. **$695**

China buffet is the current name for a combination buffet and china cabinet that incorporates features of both. In addition to a glass-enclosed section for the display of the family's choice glass and chinaware, it has a combination of drawers and doors. The glass section can be positioned in a variety of places.

China buffet with serpentine drawers, two swell-projection drawers, and convex glass door; 46" wide, 20" deep, 40" high. **$425**

Sometimes it is in the "belly" of the buffet or at one of the sides. In some rarer examples two glass sections flank the central drawer and door section. Because these pieces are not too common, they command high prices.

China cabinets are, perhaps, the most popular type of dining room storage unit. Their primary purpose is to display and store a family's prized glass and china. Some could be examples of the cups, plates, and saucers that were decorated in china painting classes that were popular in the early 1900s. Many of these were given as gifts and found cherished places in the china cabinet. The glass panels for these cabinets could be flat, concave (bent inward), or convex (rounded outward). Of the three types of glass, convex is the most common. These curved surfaces were called "bent glass" in early twentieth-century catalogs.

China cabinet with hooded top, convex glass side panels, and paw feet; 39" wide, 14" deep, 75" high. **$1,895**

China cabinet with convex glass in door and side panels and scroll feet; 44" wide, 17" deep, 64" high. **$595**

China cabinet with convex glass in door and side panels and paw feet; 42" wide, 14" deep, 66" high. **$725**

China cabinet with applied decorations and paw feet; 42" wide, 15" deep, 64" high. **$925**

China cabinet with convex glass in door and side panels; 40" wide, 14" deep, 63" high. **$725**

China cabinet; 40" wide, 12" deep, 63" high. **$575**

China cabinet with scroll pillars, a style called "colonial" in the catalogs of the 1920s; 44" wide, 14" deep, 51" high. **$475**

China cabinet with convex glass in side panels and a straight glass door with muntins; 52" wide, 14" deep, 55" high. **$775**

China cabinet with beading across top; 39" wide, 13" deep, 49" high. **$565**

China cabinet with fretwork at top of flat glass doors and scroll feet; 40" wide, 13" deep, 58" high. **$650**

China cabinet with leaded glass at top of straight glass doors; 40" wide, 13" deep, 60" high. **$775**

Corner cupboards fit into a corner of a room. Electrical outlets, heating units, doors, windows, and other structural devices make this difficult, at times, to achieve. Take a measuring tape when you go to buy an article of furniture so that you can be sure that the corner cupboard, for example, will fit into the corner you have selected.

Certain structural features built into cabinets, buffets, and sideboards tend to enhance their value. A list of them follows.

1. *Applied decorations,* including leaf garlands, scrolls, urns, and medallions, are made separately and secured to a piece.

2. Figures of animals or people that are mixed with flowers, fruits, or foilage in an unnatural way are called *grotesques.* They may be applied or carved into the piece.

3. *Projection drawers* extend out over the rest of the base.

4. *Serpentine drawers* curve in and out.

5. *Pilasters* are actually pillars sliced in half lengthwise and applied to the piece of furniture.

6. *Scroll columns* and *feet* resembled the Empire style of the early 1800s and were called "Colonial" by furniture manufacturers in the 1920s.

7. A female figure, called a *caryatid,* serves as a supporting column.

8. A male figure, called an *atlantis,* serves as a supporting column.

9. *Paw feet* are similar to an animal's paw.

10. *Claw feet* can be characterized by an eagle's talons. One type features claws clutching a ball.

11. *Cast brass hardware* pieces are used for drawer pulls, knobs, and so forth.

Corner cupboard with chamfered stiles; 45" wide, 20" deep, 97" high—too high for most modern homes. **$925**

Corner cupboard with glass panels that were originally wooden; 36" wide, 20" deep, 89" high. **$975**

China cabinet with convex glass in door and side panels and scroll feet, a style called "colonial" in the catalogs of the 1920s; 37" wide, 15" deep, 61" high. **$1,145**

Close up of a grotesque design found on a sideboard.

CHAPTER 5
Chairs and Benches

While some types of chairs are shown in Chapter 3, in what section of a home do chairs and benches actually belong? With perhaps a few exceptions, they fit into almost any setting. Because of this, and to help readers locate and compare them readily, chairs and benches rate a chapter of their own. As a further aid, chairs have been placed in categories.

Pressed-back chairs feature designs that resemble carving pressed into the wood by a metal die or mold. Mail-order catalogs extolled the "beautifully carved and embossed panels." Sometimes extra depth was added with a cutting tool. A collection of catalogs from the private library of a national wholesale furniture distributor, the agent for scores of companies, was examined. Emphasis was placed on a fifty-year span from the 1890s through the 1940s. This research revealed that pressed-back designs were abundant in the 1890s. By 1910 few were featured, and five years later the catalogs were devoid of pressed-back chairs.

Sears, Roebuck and Company and Montgomery Ward catalogs also were perused, as were catalogs from Evansville, Indiana. The library in Grand Rapids, Michigan, provided much research assistance, and their rare book room was unlocked for the authors to conduct further research.

Railroad waiting room bench with back-to-back double seat, applied flower medallion decoration above legs, and pierced designs on back and seat; 72" wide. **$650**

Solid-seat chair, set of 6. **$120** *each.*

Double-pressed-back cane-seat chair with fish design on back, set of 6. **$260** *each*

Close-up of fish design on chair back. Elaborate patterns such as this one are unusual and add to a chair's price.

Pressed-back chair, set of 4. **$150** *each*

Double-pressed-back cane-seat armchair with fish design on back, set of 6. **$280** *each*

Pressed-back chair, set of 6. **$150** *each*

Double-pressed-back cane-seat chair, set of 6. **$175** *each*

Triple-pressed-back cane-seat chair, set of 6. **$245** *each*

Pressed-back solid-seat chair with Man of the North Wind design, set of 6. **$250** *each*

Close-up of Man of the North Wind.

Pressed-back cane-seat chair, set of 6. **$170** *each*

Pressed-back solid-seat chair with impressed designs on the front corners of the chair seat. **$180**

Pressed-back solid-seat chair, set of 4. **$135** *each*

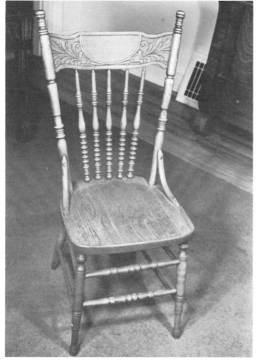

Pressed-back solid-seat chair, set of 4. **$135** *each*

Pressed-back cane-seat chair, set of 4. **$170** *each*

Pressed-back chair with cane seat, set of 4. **$595**

Pressed-back solid-seat chair with turnings that resemble stacks of coins, set of 6. **$170** *each*

Pressed-back cane-seat chair with serpentlike medallion on back, set of 4. **$185** *each*

Close up of serpentlike medallion on chair back.

Generally, the more elaborate designs appeared on the earlier chairs. There could be single, double, triple, or quadruple pressing on the surface. Single pressings are found on the top rail. The multiple designs might be present on chairs with two or three back slats (horizontal cross pieces); on a back splat (central upright); or, if a seat had an apron beneath it, a pressed design could be there. In a very few instances a pattern is found on the corners of a seat. Garlands, scrolls, flowerlike patterns, or circle outlines with seemingly endless variations are present. It is less common to see such designs as a man blowing (now called Man of the North Wind), serpents, birds, fish, and what appears to be mermaids on chair backs. A high chair graced with Mother Goose is appropriate for a child.

Pressed-back cane-seat chair. **$210**

Pressed-back chair with unusual pressed design on the seat around the cane, set of 2. **$350** *each*

Double-pressed-back cane-seat chair. **$290**

53

Double-pressed-back chair. **$185**

Triple-pressed-back chair, set of 2. **$295** *each*

Triple-pressed-back cane-seat chair. **$260**

A group of pressed designs are pictured here in order to illustrate the variety of patterns available.

Cane seats were used on many pressed-back chairs instead of solid wooden seats. Most of the cane was the pressed variety, cut to size, wetted, and pressed into a glued groove on the chair's seat. An earlier type had holes drilled around the periphery of the seat. Six steps of hand weaving and a seventh binding step were necessary in order to make a hand-caned seat.

Pressed-back cane-seat chair, set of 4. **$140** *each*

Pressed-back cane-seat chair, set of 6. **$140** *each*

Pressed-back cane-seat chair, set of 4. **$140** *each*

Spindle-back cane-seat chair, set of 4. **$165** *each*

61

Spindle-back cane-seat chair, set of 6. **$140** *each*

Splat-back or T-back chair, set of 6. **$95** *each*

T-backs were introduced in the 1920s and 1930s and then were known as splat-back chairs. Because this vertical splat resembles the letter "T" when it joins the back rail, it has been nicknamed a "T-back."

Windsor chairs that featured turned spindles were common after 1920. This style may have originated near England's Windsor Castle in the early 1700s and arrived in the Philadelphia area after 1725. In approximately thirty-five years Windsors became the predominant chair. They featured graceful, multispindled backs and splayed legs that pierced the seats. Pictured in this chapter is a Windsor style bench, a copy of this early design.

The bar stool or captain's chair found on boats, in club rooms, or in other casual settings is often referred to as a "debased" Windsor.

Splat-back or T-back leather-seat chair, set of 4. **$90** *each*

Splat-back or T-back upholstered-seat chair, set of 6.
$90 *each*

Bentwood chairs were developed by Michael Thonet of Austria around 1840. He used steam-bent wooden rods and mass-produced aesthetically pleasing furniture that was light but durable. Similar styles of furniture continue to be made today.

Mission style examples can be found in Chapter 10 and in the color section.

Heywood-Wakefield was the result of the merger of two furniture-making titans. In the 1840s Cyrus Wakefield and Levi Heywood were competitors who each made wicker furniture. After both men died their rival companies merged in 1897 as Heywood Brothers and Wakefield Company. The name later was simplified to Heywood-Wakefield. The company closed its wood furniture division in 1979. One chair from a set of cane chairs with Heywood-Wakefield labels is shown on page 64.

Windsor-type bench with splayed legs and H stretcher; 39" wide, 17" deep, 36" high. **$450**

Round-seat chair with cabriole legs and bentwood hoop stretcher that pierces front legs; 22" arm to arm, 30" high. **$225**

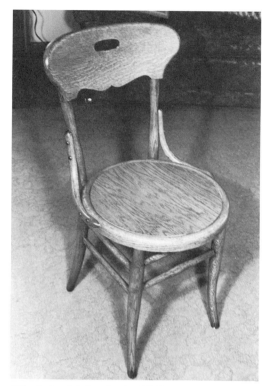

Side chair with hand grip. **$100**

Heywood-Wakefield cane-seat chair, set of 4. **$300**

Bentwood cane-seat armchair; 22" arm to arm, 35" high, set of 2. **$150**

Settee; 46" wide, 18" deep, 35" high. **$480**

CHAPTER 6
The Kitchen

A cookstove, storage cupboards, a refrigerator (icebox), and table are furnishings that make up a kitchen.

The old black cast-iron kitchen range that devoured corncobs, chips, coal, and wood was an all-purpose unit in the early twentieth-century kitchen. By 1929 the Montgomery Ward catalog pictured gas-, oil-, kerosene-, and gasoline-burning ranges that came in a variety of colors: spring green, french gray, ivory tan, and turquoise blue. Many had less bulky lines than the black kitchen stove and stood on tall legs, but the old range continued to be advertised.

The *Hoosier-type cabinets* that collectors purchase today were first illustrated in a turn-of-the-century catalog. The name was derived from the fact that many of these cabinets were made in Indiana, the Hoosier state. The Hoosier Manufacturing Company of New Castle, Indiana, gave the name Hoosier to the cabinets. Because many other companies provided similar examples, these have come to be labeled "Hoosier-type" cabinets.

A 1929 catalog advertised these popular units as being available in five beautiful new colors: "Warm Golden Oak, Snowflake White, Modern French Gray, Rich Old Ivory or New Spring Green."

Hoosier kitchen cabinet, made in New Castle, Ind., with side-moving tambour doors, porcelain pullout working surface, and an oval zinc label at the top reading "The Hoosier Saves Steps"; 42" wide, 25" deep, 71" high. **$645**

The Housekeeper's Food Guide found inside the door in the Hoosier cabinet.

Hoosier-type kitchen cabinet with a pull-down tambour door, porcelain pullout working surface, and original floral designs on three doors with a plaque on front reading "Sellers Kitchen Cabinet, Elwood, Indiana"; 40" wide, 26" deep, 70" high. **$600**

Hoosier-type kitchen cabinet, circa 1930s, with white factory finish, pull-down tambour door, porcelain pull-out working surface, and a label reading "Ingram Richardson Mfg. Co., Frankfort, Ind."; 40" wide, 25" deep, 71" high. **$350**

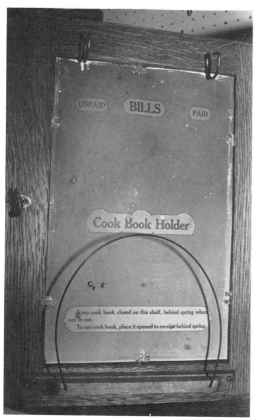

A Cook Book Holder found inside a Hoosier-type cabinet marked "Napanee Dutch Kitchenet, pat. Feb. 24, 1914."

Metal holders for extracts and other miscellaneous items found inside a Hoosier-type cabinet marked "Napanee Dutch Kitchenet, pat. Feb. 24, 1914."

Other known Indiana "Hoosier-type cabinet" producers were the Sellers Company of Elwood, Ingram Richardson Manufacturing Company of Frankfort, Wasmuth Endicott Company of Andrews, Napanee Dutch Kitchenet of Nappanee, and the Boone and Greencastle Companies. In Iowa the Hawkeye cabinet was made by Union Furniture Company of Burlington. Scheirich and Com-

Hoosier-type kitchen cabinet with three colored glass panels, pull-down tambour door, flour sifter, porcelain pullout working surface, and a label reading "Sellers The Better Kitchen Cabinet Kitchen Maid, Elwood, Ind., U. S. A. Trademark registered"; 41" wide, 27" deep, 70" high. **$750**

pany of Louisville, Kentucky, brought out this type of kitchen unit while the Wilson Kitchen Cabinet originated in Grand Rapids, Michigan. Whenever possible, look for and preserve company names on brass tags or metal handles, instruction cards, or any shipping information on the back of these cabinets.

Noteworthy features of Hoosiers or Hoosier-types, which were advertised to save space, time, steps, and drudgery, are many. Metal-lined bread drawers; drop-down flour bins and sugar containers; built-in sifters; pull-out boards for kneading and chopping, and storage sections for pots, pans, china, and cooking utensils are included. Tea, coffee, and other essentials could line the top shelf. A porcelain, zinc, or wooden work surface, on which the upper section rested, could be pulled out to provide a larger work area.

Hoosier-type kitchen cabinet with a pull-down tambour door and a pullout cutting board with breadboard ends; 40" wide, 24" deep, 69" high. **$595**

Hoosier-type kitchen cabinet that was used as an all-in-one unit for a baby. A quilted pad over porcelain pullout working surface was used for diaper changing, the flour bin housed the diapers, food was kept behind the pull-down tambour door, and other drawers held blankets and clothing; 40" wide, 27" deep, 69" high. **$645**

Kitchen cabinet; 42" wide, 24" deep, 77" high. **$1,195**

Hoosier-type kitchen cabinet with a pull-down tambour door, porcelain pullout working surface, metal bread box and sifter, identified as "June Bride," manufactured by Sellers; 41" wide, 25" deep, 70" high. **$625**

Other types of cupboards were available as well. In today's terminology a *closed cupboard* has wooden doors. *Open cupboards* have glass doors at the top or open shelves without doors. *Straight fronts* are cabinets vertically straight without any breaks. The base projects out further than the top on a *step-back cupboard*.

Step-back kitchen cabinet with incised lines; 40" wide, 19" deep, 84" high. **$695**

These cupboards were advertised as mouse-proof and sanitary. Some had a flexible door, called a tambour, that operated in grooves. It was made of strips of wood attached to a canvas or duck backing. Some opened vertically while others pulled across horizontally.

For economy's sake it was possible to purchase a base only. In addition, "Budget Plan Terms" permitted payments of so much down and so much per month with a small service fee added. Buying on time became increasingly popular in the 1920s.

A man who formerly was employed by the New Castle Hoosier Cabinet factory stated that their market ceased in the 1940s when built-in features became standard in homes.

Two-piece step-back kitchen cabinet with incised lines; 40" wide, 19" deep, 84" high. **$750**

One-piece kitchen cabinet with glass doors in upper section; 37" wide, 16" deep, 73" high. **$575**

One-piece kitchen cabinet with glass doors in upper section; 36" wide, 14" deep, 74" high. **$675**

Pie shelf is another term used. In this version there is a small open space between the top and the base where pies could be set to cool.

Rectangular or round extension tables were customarily a part of a large kitchen. For convenience such tables are grouped together in Chapter 4. Only the drop-leaf table and a worktable were selected for kitchen duty in this chapter.

Kitchen worktable, dated Jan. 6, 1941 in drawer; 42" wide, 25" deep, 30" high. **$295**

Food preservation presented a problem. Catalogs from the past used the word "refrigerator" when referring to what today is termed an icebox. It is interesting to note that the so-called oak *icebox* often was made of ash, elm, or northern hardwoods. These were still available in 1929, but a new feature was present. Porcelain-lined refrigerators with 1 1/2" corkboard insulation and outside cases finished in "glistening white enamel over polished steel" came "equipped with hanger bolts and sleeve openings to take electrical refrigeration units if desired." Otherwise, an ice compartment was present.

Drop-leaf extension table with two 12" leaves; 29" by 43", 30" high, 13" drop leaves, with four accompanying chairs that are not pictured. **$595** *for the set*

Oval drop-leaf table; 41" by 22", 31" high, 13" drop leaves. **$325**

Icebox, currently in use, with a label reading "Lapland Monitor, The Ramey Refrigerator Co., Greenville, Mich."; 35" wide, 20" deep, 48" high. **$625**

Icebox with zinc interior intact; 26" wide, 19" deep, 48" high. **$450**

Icebox with lift lid for ice compartment, molded panels, and a label reading "Cold Storage"; 28" wide, 17" deep, 43" high. **$475**

Icebox with a label reading "American House Furnishing Co."; 21" wide, 14" deep, 37" high. **$475**

When rural areas became electrified, farmers no longer had to saw blocks of ice from frozen rivers in winter to keep perishables cool in summer. Ice blocks were stored in an old unused building where sand or sawdust separated layers of blocks and helped insulate the icehouse. All those who cooperated in the ice-cutting operation had free access to the ice supply for summertime use. In town, housewives put out a card to indicate how much ice the iceman should leave when his wagon or truck cruised through the neighborhood. Children liked to find small slivers of ice on the truck to suck in hot weather. These happenings would soon belong to the past.

Before water was piped into homes, it was brought inside in buckets from a well. In such cases, there was no bathroom in which to hang *medicine chests*. Therefore, a small version was hung in the kitchen. In addition to holding medicines, a man's shaving soap and folding straight razor were kept there. His "strop" for sharpening the blade hung nearby and the basin for water was readily available.

Another hanging kitchen accessory was the *spice cabinet,* with its multiple drawers to hold various seeds, leaves, and spice sticks.

The kitchen was the center of the home. Children did school projects on the table or played games while sitting there. And, of course, the tub for the Saturday night bath was hauled into the kitchen, and each member of the family took a turn getting clean. Electricity and plumbing would soon change all of this.

Medicine chest; 15" wide, 6" deep, 19" high. **$185**

Medicine chest; 17" wide, 6" deep, 28" high. **$185**

Spice box. **$195**

74

CHAPTER 7
The Children's Room

Children's items are bought by parents who enjoy nostalgic objects or by indulgent grandparents who seek usable, "time-was" articles. Collectors like to find miniature pieces of furniture so they can put their dolls on display in natural settings and poses. *High chairs, small tables,* and *chairs, beds,* and other wee furniture are sought. Most popular with these collectors are swing *cradles* or those on platforms.

Toys from the past are hunted and collected by adult buyers. Women who enjoy unusual decor or perhaps a country or Victorian flavor purchase children's things as well.

Some examples of pressed-back chairs and rockers are available in children's sizes. In addition, mission-style furniture was made with children in mind.

Since patented furniture was popular in the late 1800s and early 1900s, children were not neglected. High chairs had dual purposes—they could be converted into go-carts or collapsed to form rocking chairs. Terminology differed slightly—the tray was referred to as a table. In current usage, the go-cart is called a stroller.

Children's desks emulated the adult versions. A fall-front rolltop, with its one curve reminiscent of the letter C, is pictured on page 78. An unusual draw table has been made to accommodate children.

Hunting for children's furniture is a never-ending adventure.

Pressed-back cane-seat high chair go-cart combination; 17" wide, 19" deep, 41" high. **$550**

Cane-seat high chair go-cart combination; 42" high.
$450

High chair with T-back and splayed legs; 18" wide, 39" high. **$250**

Pressed-back cane-seat high chair; 42" high. **$225**

High chair converted into youth chair; 41" high. **$170**

Child's pressed-back rocker; 28" high. **$200**

Child's pressed-back rocker; 28" high. **$150**

Child's rocker; 28" high. **$150**

Child's mission rocker; 26" high. **$165**

Child's rocker; 21" arm to arm, 29" high. **$150**

Child's drop-lid desk with applied decorations and flower cutouts on the sides; 22" wide, 11" deep, 33" high. **$210**

Child's C-curve rolltop desk; 26" wide, 16" deep, 37" high. **$225**

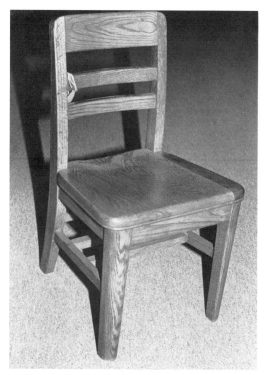

Child's slat-back chair that could be used with child's desk; 26" high. **$45**

Draw table that could have been an apprentice piece, a salesman's sample, or a child's table; 26" wide, 16" deep, 22" high, 8" draw leaves. **$215**

Baby bed; 22" wide, 39" long, 25" high. **$365**

Mission doll's bed; 13" wide, 22" deep, 11" high. **$135**

Cradle on platform; 21" wide, 39" long, 33" high. **$370**

Cradle on platform with applied decorations; 23" wide, 42" long, 46" high. **$695**

Child's chiffonier or chest of drawers with swing mirror; 22" wide, 15" deep, 58" high. **$575**

Child's "Teddy" wagon with orange spoke wheels and slats that form its bed; 14" wide, 36" deep. **$475**

Child's one-piece kitchen cabinet; 22" wide, 11" deep, 40" high. **$425**

CHAPTER 8
The Study and Music Room

A dual-purpose room for study and music is actually a hypothetical space. Most residences did not boast such a combination, and in wealthy homes the two would be in separate, spacious areas. Indeed, a mid-income house might have some but not all of the furniture listed and pictured in this chapter. For example, a library table, phonograph, or piano might be the only "extras" an average room could hold in addition to the necessary table and seating arrangements. In fact, in an average home, some of these pieces would occupy space in the living room.

Consider first what furnishings are desirable in a study or home office. A desk and its accompanying chair, bookcase, and file cabinet generally rank as essentials.

Office armchair. $175

Bookcase with adjustable shelves, currently used to store and display china and glass; 39" wide, 14" deep, 57" high. $545

S-curve rolltop desk and another roll on the left side of the kneehole with a pullout shelf; 55" wide, 34" deep, 53" high. **$2,300**

File cabinet with 36 drawers, originally used in the University of Iowa library; 42" wide, 17" deep, 35" high. **$900**

Double-section bookcase with rolled waterfall-type top and paw feet; 44" wide, 13" deep, 59" high. **$795**

Bookcases from the late 1800s could be tall and elegant with incised carving, applied decorations, and carved cornices in the East-lake style. Much-later bookcases with a rounded top edge represent the waterfall style that was marketed mainly in the late 1930s through the early 1950s.

Bookcase with plank sides, incised lines, and carved cornice. Original owner purchased this with his first month's pay as a schoolteacher; 42" wide, 12" deep, 81" high. **$1,150**

Bookcase with open and closed storage space; 27" wide, 12" deep, 53" high. **$535**

Bookcase with applied decorations; 41" wide, 13" deep, 78" high. **$1,100**

Bookcase with applied beading around glass door panels, circa 1920s; 39" wide, 15" deep, 62" high. **$675**

Bookcase; 48" wide, 13" deep, 51" high. **$895**

Bookshelf with three slatted shelves; 20" wide, 13" deep, 38" high. **$105**

A bookcase that could grow as a family's library expanded was the sectional bookcase. The Gunn Company, a Grand Rapids firm, patented one in 1899. Others were made by Globe-Wernicke of Cincinnati, Ohio, and Macey of Grand Rapids, Michigan. In 1902 Sears offered a Bauch extension bookcase that could be shipped knocked down to save on freight expenses. Upon its arrival it could be assembled easily. The glass-fronted doors, which slid on roller bearings for easy operation, made the book titles easily visible. The doors pulled up and pushed into the case when opened. Each rectangular section was purchased separately and was stacked on top of another. A top and base were individual units. Leaded glass occasionally added a decorative touch, and five or six sections were the norm.

Stack bookcase in five sections with doors that pull up and slide in; 34" wide, 12" deep, 47" high. **$450**

Stack bookcase with doors that pull up and slide in, originally finished in fumed oak, in six sections with leaded glass in the upper section and a label reading "Gunn Sectional Bookcase, pat., Dec. 5, 1899; June 1, 1901, Grand Rapids"; 34" wide, 12" deep, 66" high. **$825**

Stack bookcase in six sections with doors that pull up and slide in, used as a china cabinet; 34" wide, 14" deep, 56" high. **$650**

Stack bookcase in five sections with doors that pull up and slide in; 34" wide, 13" deep, 43" high. **$525**

Stack bookcase in five sections with doors that pull up and slide in; 34" wide, 11" deep, 51" high. **$475**

Desks came in many styles. One version had various names, including *combination bookcase-desk, bookcase-secretary, side-by-side,* or *library case and secretary.* These can be plain with uncluttered lines or have applied or carved decorations, mirrors, shelves, and ornamental feet. The glass-enclosed bookcase had either straight or convex glass panels or a combination of the two. The convex glass that curves out was called bent glass in the early twentieth-century catalogs.

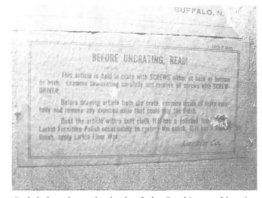

Label found on the back of the Larkin combination bookcase-desk.

Combination bookcase-desk with incised carving; 39" wide, 14" deep, 67" high. **$725**

Combination bookcase-desk; 38" wide, 14" deep, 65" high. **$475**

Combination bookcase-desk with applied decorations and incised carving; 39" wide, 13" deep, 68" high. **$725**

Combination bookcase-desk supplied by Larkin Company; 42" wide, 14" deep, 67" high. **$1,450**

Combination bookcase-desk with convex glass door panel, projection swell drawer and applied decorations; 37" wide, 12" deep, 68" high. **$725**

Combination bookcase-desk with incised decorations; 38" wide, 12" deep, 67" high. **$995**

Combination bookcase-desk with convex glass door panel, leaded glass door over drop lid, pillar stiles, paw feet, and a label on the back reading "Factory #13, Larkin Co., Buffalo, N. Y.—Mr. C. Johnson to Moline, Illinois." **$1,745**

Combination bookcase-desk with convex glass door panel, applied decorations, and hood over desk area; 42" wide, 13" deep, 76" high. **$1,850**

Combination bookcase-desk with applied decorations; 43" wide, 13" deep, 75" high. **$795**

Combination left-handed-style bookcase-desk with incised decorations; 41" wide, 12" deep, 73" high. **$910**

Most of these cases are meant to accommodate right-handed writers. The drop-lid desk section is on the right, the bookcase to the left. This enabled the user to reach with the left hand to secure a book. When the desk is to the left, a left-hander could keep his paper and pen ready as he reached to his right.

Combination left-handed-style bookcase-desk with incised and applied decorations and swing mirror; 46" wide, 14" deep, 73" high. **$995**

Those that had a central writing section flanked by bookcases also were available, but they were scarcer. Behind the fall-front lid in all of these desks was storage space, most frequently a combination of small drawers and slots.

Another common type of secretary has a bookcase section above the desk. On many of these a rounded hood or cylinder covered the work surface when it was not in use. It was a solid, continuous roll, not a slatted device. Such secretaries also came with fall or drop fronts.

Fall-front secretary with applied decorations; 38" wide, 18" deep, 85" high. **$1,095**

Cylinder secretary with applied carving; 38" wide, 22" deep, 85" high. **$1,950**

A *rolltop* differs from the solid hood cylinder because it is made of horizontal, parallel, flexible slats of wood that are glued to a canvas, duck, or linen backing. The roll can be either the more-desirable S curve or the C curve.

S-curve rolltop desk; 50" wide, 34" deep, 46" high. **$2,400**

S-curve rolltop desk; 48" wide, 31" deep, 48" high. **$1,950**

S-curve rolltop desk; 46" wide, 36" deep, 46" high. **$4,250**

C-curve rolltop desk; 36" wide, 28" deep, 44" high. **$875**

S-curve rolltop desk; 65" wide, 36" deep, 50" high. **$6,800**

S-curve rolltop desk with a patent date of 1884; 60" wide, 34" deep, 51" high. **$5,750**

A desk with a drop-down lid for writing is referred to as a *drop front* or *fall front*. When these slant in at the top, it is labeled a slant front. Small desks that often had such a feature were frequently referred to as parlor desks. Of course, the side-by-side desk already mentioned is an example of the fall-front style.

Fall-front desk that was originally a part of a side-by-side or combination bookcase-desk, with pressed designs; 22" wide, 14" deep, 41" high. **$375**

Fall-front parlor desk with swell drawer fronts; 30" wide, 17" deep, 50" high. **$525**

Fall-front parlor or lady's desk with applied decorations; 25" wide, 12" deep, 42" high. **$325**

Lady's desks are customarily dainty. Fall-front examples often have only one drawer under the writing area and stand tall on long, spindly legs that may be cabriole in style.

Fall-front parlor or lady's desk with swell drawer and applied decorations; 26" wide, 14" deep, 48" high. **$395**

Fall-front parlor desk with serpentine lid, applied decorations, and grotesque figure; 30" wide, 17" deep, 42" high. **$595**

Fall-front desk with applied decorations and a metal rail; 26" wide, 17" deep, 38" high. **$595**

Decorative touches on desks included grotesques, figures or partial figures of animals or people mixed with flowers, fruit, or foliage in a fantastic fashion; serpentine lines that wiggle in and out like a snake in motion; drawers that swell out; or other ornamentation. Common finishes were golden and fumed oak.

An office desk could be called a *single pedestal desk* when there was a kneehole opening beneath for the user's legs and drawers on one side. A double pedestal meant that there were drawers on each side of the kneehole center section.

Double-pedestal kneehole office desk that is paneled on the back so it can be positioned as a room divider; 53" wide, 25" deep, 30" high. **$595**

Desk with shelves on each side for book or magazine storage; 38" wide, 24" deep, 30" high. **$195**

Single-pedestal kneehole office desk; 36" wide, 27" deep, 31" high. **$395**

Naturally *office chairs* that have motion are desirable. They swivel, tilt back, glide across the floor on rollers, and some can be adjusted in height. Both wooden- and cane-seat versions are available. Sometimes the backs also are caned. The more common variety are stationary armchairs.

Swivel office chair; 24" arm to arm. **$175**

Swivel pressed-back cane-seat chair; 22" arm to arm, 42" high. **$425**

Armchair with cane seat and back; 21" arm to arm, 36" high. **$300**

Swivel office chair; 24" arm to arm. **$175**

Swivel cane-seat chair; 22" arm to arm, 41" high.
$375

Office armchair with handhold in back rail. **$175**

Swivel cane-seat chair; 22" arm to arm, 43" high.
$375

Office armchair. **$175**

Office armchair. **$125**

File cabinets, an office aid, are now adopted by the younger set to house VCR tapes and cassettes. They also retain their useful, old-fashioned function of keeping official papers filed in a systematic manner.

File cabinet, originally property of the United States Army Air Force; 20" wide, 25" deep, 53" high. **$350**

File cabinet with four drawers; 13" wide, 16" deep 9" high. **$150**

Organs of yore frequently had shelves to hold lamps. The musician had to pump up and down with the feet as the hands glided over the keys and pulled out the proper stops to produce the desired sounds. Knee action was required, too. An organ stool supported the player.

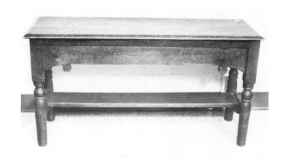

Piano bench with lift lid; 41" wide, 14" deep, 21" high. **$135**

Epworth organ made by Williams Organ Co., Chicago, Ill.; 55" wide, 30" deep, 47" high. **$895**

Either a rectangular *piano bench,* which usually had a lift-lid storage section where the music was kept, or a piano stool that could be raised or lowered, provided the seat for the musician.

Piano stool; 15" diameter, 21" high as pictured. **$165**

Piano bench converted into a coffee table; 39" wide, 19" deep, 21" high. **$135**

Music cabinets had various designs within to hold many kinds of music paraphernalia such as sheet music, piano rolls for player pianos, or records for phonographs.

Music cabinet used to store sheet music, records, or player piano rolls; 18" wide, 16" deep, 34" high. **$175**

Victrola made by Victor Talking Machine Co., sold by Stack Piano Co., Chicago, Ill. **$325**

Thomas A. Edison created his favorite invention, the first successful *talking machine*, in 1877. It was operated by a hand crank and enabled the human voice to be heard on records. Both the floor and tabletop varieties brought music into thousands of homes. The first words he quoted and heard repeated on his tin-foil-covered cylinder were from the poem "Mary Had a Little Lamb," written by *Godey's Lady's Book* editor Sarah Josepha Hale.

Edison phonograph with latest patent date of Nov. 17, 1903; 13" wide, 9" deep, 12" high. **$625**

*Graphophone made by Columbia Phonograph Co., with latest patent date of March 30, 1897; 12"
wide, 8" deep, 7" high.* **$650**

CHAPTER 9
The Bedroom

In the late 1800s the *bed* served a person from the cradle to the grave. Customarily babies were born in the home, and when people were extremely ill they generally were cared for in their own bedrooms. Doctors made house calls to provide medical assistance.

Since bathrooms were not common in the early 1900s and a back path led to the necessary building outdoors, the bedroom needed special nighttime accommodations. A potty with a lid peeked shyly out from under the bed, ready if required.

Bed with applied decorations; 57" wide (lengthened to 84"), 57" high headboard, 37" high footboard.
$475

Bed with applied decorations; 59" wide, 79" long, 60" high headboard. **$475**

A *washstand commode* with its combination of drawers and doors could have a towel bar on top. Hidden within this piece was the lidded slop jar. A washbowl and large pitcher for personal cleansing sat primly on top, along with other parts of the chamber set such as a toothbrush holder, lidded soap dish, and a smaller pitcher. Hot and cold water were not delivered by pipes to a faucet. Instead, family members or servants carried water to the rooms in pitchers. Woe to anyone who left water in a ceramic receptacle on a crisp winter night. By morning it might be covered with ice in the unheated bedroom.

Washstand commode with incised lines; 30" wide, 17" deep, 30" high. **$275**

Single bed with applied decorations; 40" wide, 76" long. **$375**

Washstand commode with incised lines and spoon carving; 32" wide, 19" deep, 36" high. **$350**

Washstand commode with towel bar removed but available; 33" wide, 17" deep, 26" high. **$275**

Washstand commode with applied decorations, projection serpentine drawer, and towel bar back; 34" wide, 20" deep, 53" high. **$345**

Washstand commode with projection serpentine drawer and towel bar back; 33" wide, 19" deep, 56" high. **$275**

Marble-top washstand commode with incised lines and designs; 32" wide, 18" deep, 28" high. **$450**

Washstand commode with incised lines and spoon carving designs; 30" wide, 17" deep, 30" high. **$295**

Washstand commode with towel bar back; 36" wide, 19" deep, 44" high. **$300**

Marble-top washstand commode with incised lines; 32" wide, 17" deep, 34" high. **$450**

Small washstands with one drawer, a lower shelf, and towel bar ends were manufactured in oak or other woods. These served as inexpensive chamber set holders.

The bedroom set included a bedstead and dresser in addition to the washing sites already mentioned.

Washstand commode with projection serpentine drawer and swing mirror; 32" wide, 18" deep, 52" high. **$365**

Three-piece bedroom set with applied decorations and incised lines. Bed is 64" wide, 73" high headboard, 33" high footboard; dresser is 43" wide, 19" deep, 73" high; washstand is 32" wide, 15" deep, 37" high. **$3,900** *for set*

In 1897 the Sears and Roebuck catalog advertised an "elegant solid oak bedroom suite" with hand carving for $16.00. It was accompanied by a *chevalle (cheval) dresser* with a large imported beveled mirror. Alongside it, a hat cabinet with two small drawers shared the top of the two-drawer base. The bed was 6 feet tall, while the dresser with its elongated mirror towered to 6' 6". Included in this set was a commode and its accompanying mirror.

Cheval dresser with hat cabinet, incised lines, and decorations; 48" wide, 21" deep, 82" high. **$595**

Cheval dresser with hat cabinet and applied decorations; 42" wide, 21" deep, 76" high. **$675**

Cheval mirror used for shaving and makeup; 20" wide, 9" deep, 25" high. **$225**

The more common style of dresser that accompanied a bedroom set featured a series of drawers and a swing mirror. The top two drawers were generally small. An ash dresser typical of what could be purchased in the latter part of the nineteenth century is illustrated to show the contrast in styles. A dressing table or vanity was sometimes part of a set.

Dresser with swing mirror; 42" wide, 20" deep, 65" high. **$275**

Dresser with applied decorations, swing mirror, and serpentine drawers; 40" wide, 20" deep, 84" high. **$390**

Dresser with applied decorations and swing mirror; 44" wide, 22" deep, 76" high. **$375**

Dresser with applied decorations, serpentine drawers, and swing mirror; 42" wide, 20" deep, 77" high. **$425**

Dresser with applied decorations, triple mirror, and serpentine drawers; 42" wide, 22" deep, 73" high. **$695**

Dresser with applied decorations, swing mirror, and serpentine drawers; 41" wide, 19" deep, 72" high. **$455**

Dresser with applied decorations and swing mirror; 40" wide, 19" deep, 70" high. **$375**

Princess dresser with swell projection center drawer and swing mirror; 42" wide, 20" deep, 65" high. **$395**

Ash dresser with applied decorations and wishbone mirror; 41" wide, 19" deep, 77" high. **$750**

Dressing table with applied decorations, small swell drawers, cabriole legs, and swing mirror; 40" wide, 22" deep, 66" high. **$995**

Princess dresser with applied decorations, serpentine drawers, and swing mirror; 40" wide, 21" deep, 71" high. **$395**

"Princess" has a dainty, regal sound. A princess dresser was low, generally with petite, graceful lines and either two long drawers below a generous swing mirror or a combination of two small parallel drawers and one long drawer. This style remains popular today.

Princess dresser with applied decorations, serpentine drawers, and swing mirror; 42" wide, 22" deep, 68" high. **$330**

Princess dresser with applied decorations and swing mirror; 41" wide, 21" deep, 73" high. **$395**

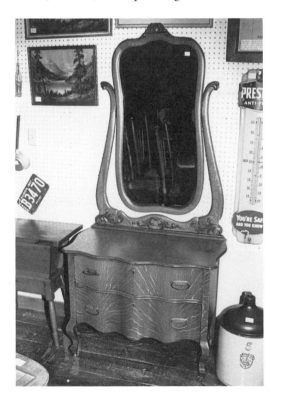

Chiffoniers were tall chests of drawers with or without mirrors. Owners today tend to call them highboys instead. Some incorporated a hatbox.

Chiffonier with serpentine drawers and door, hat cabinet, and cabriole legs; 34" wide, 18" deep, 48" high. **$465**

Princess dresser with applied decorations, serpentine drawers, and swing mirror; 34" wide, 19" deep, 70" high. **$375**

113

Chiffonier with pilasters separating swell top drawers and door and paw feet; 42" wide, 22" deep, 47" high. **$475**

Chiffonier with serpentine drawers; 30" wide, 19" deep, 40" high. **$395**

Chiffonier with incised lines; 33" wide, 18" deep, 41" high. **$425**

Chiffonier with swell drawer fronts; 35" wide, 18" deep, 50" high. **$365**

Chiffonier with projection serpentine top drawers; 34" wide, 18" deep, 55" high. **$385**

Chiffonier with swell front and applied decorations on back rail; 33" wide, 19" deep, 59" high. **$275**

Chiffonier with applied decorations and swing mirror; 28" wide, 17" deep, 55" high. **$350**

Chiffonier with hatbox and incised lines; 36" wide, 19" deep, 55" high. **$385**

Chiffonier with projection top drawers and swing mirror; 33" wide, 19" deep, 71" high. **$355**

Chiffonier with applied decorations and swing mirror; 33" wide, 18" deep, 72" high. **$525**

Chiffonier with scroll stiles and swing mirror supports, a style often called "colonial" in the 1920s catalogs; 36" wide, 20" deep, 69" high. **$320**

Chiffonier with applied decorations and swing mirror; 34" wide, 19" deep, 70" high. **$595**

Chifforobe with swing mirror, slide-out garment bar behind the closed door, and a fall-front desk surface; 43" wide, 19" deep, 68" high. **$525**

Because closets were lacking in most homes, it was necessary to buy furniture that provided hanging space. A *chifforobe* had drawers on one side and the closet area on the other.

Wardrobes were designed in many ways, but customarily there was a shelf at the top within and hooks and a hanging rod for garments. Some wardrobes had one door, but more often they had two. Drawer space might be included at the base of the piece. Since a wardrobe is usually large and bulky, hard to transport—and difficult to get to a top floor around narrow, winding stairs—a clever design solved this problem. Many were constructed so they were collapsible or of a knock-down design with easy-to-assemble features so they fit together snugly. Marking the various pieces when disassembling a wardrobe makes the reassembly process a lot easier.

Wardrobe with beveled mirror, applied decorations, and pillars on stiles; 55" wide, 20" deep, 88" high. **$1,250**

Ash wardrobe with incised lines and original wooden door panels replaced with glass; 40" wide, 16" deep, 78" high. $775

Wardrobe with applied decorations and original wooden door panels replaced with glass; 48" wide, 18" deep, 96" high. $950

Wardrobe converted into china cabinet by replacing wooden panels with glass and adding shelves; 42" wide, 12" deep, 68" high. $465

Wardrobe that breaks down for easier transportation; 43" wide, 17" deep, 83" high. **$1,125**

Wardrobe with incised carving; 39" wide, 16" deep, 80" high. **$775**

Wardrobe with incised carving and applied decorations; 44" wide, 16" deep, 82" high. **$825**

Ash wardrobe; 44" wide, 17" deep, 84" high. **$750**

Wardrobe with applied decorations and molded door panels; 44" wide, 17" deep, 80" high. **$795**

Wardrobes are generally not used in homes today as they were originally intended. They often function as entertainment centers to house televisions, stereos, and related articles.

An unusual bed that was not a part of a set and could be found in another part of the house was a *Murphy bed*. The terms, "combination," "mantel," and "upright" have been found in early twentieth-century catalogs to describe this old type of hide-a-bed or fold-up unit. In some elaborate types, a bed was available when in the down position, but when closed the bed was transformed into a combination wardrobe-desk. Other possibilities included a bookcase, writing desk, and bed. A safety draw bed was the name for a bed-dresser duo. But despite the use of other names, the generic term Murphy bed is retained in today's vernacular.

Murphy or mantel bed with mirror in top rail and applied decorations; 55" wide, 19" deep, 63" high. **$1,495**

It was interesting to observe that a preponderance of oak veneer pieces were offered for sale in the 1923–1924 Montgomery Ward catalog when in previous years solid oak was the predominant choice. Forest supplies of oak were dwindling, other woods and veneers were replacing oak as the dominant wood, and styles were beginning to change. Veneered bedroom sets in walnut with burl mahogany decorations were built in the Queen Anne, Adam period, and Louis XVI styles. Painted furniture and metal examples were also shown. Oak's period of prominence was beginning to ebb.

Murphy bed in open position.

CHAPTER 10

The Arts and Crafts Movement and Mission Furniture

Do you realize that the Industrial Revolution helped create a middle class of workers? Through the use of machines, the need to make articles at home by hand was replaced by the know-how to create products in factories. Formerly only the wealthy could buy certain commodities, but when factories hired workers and turned out inexpensive wares, average people became consumers.

Arts and Crafts Furniture

Let's look at some of the luminaries of the Arts and Crafts Movement.

CHARLES LOCK(E) EASTLAKE

Eastlake (1836–1906) wrote *Hints on Household Taste*, published around 1868, which promoted rectangles and squares. Victorian furniture, with its round contours, soaring heights, and ornately carved features, wasted wood. He felt that straight lines were stronger and better.

Eastlake disliked the rapidly produced, inferior commercial wares that some factories turned out with their power-driven machines. He deplored their eclectic tendency to borrow, adopt, and combine any patterns of the past and felt shoddy furniture resulted.

He liked the Japanese clean, practical, functional lines, and the delicate tracery of old Gothic patterns. Chip carving and incised parallel lines (now sometimes referred to as "railroad tracks") provided decorative touches that did not waste wood.

The furniture industry was ready for a change and wanted to promote planned designs. Thus, England's Eastlake fostered a new trend in which straight styles were fashionable. There was one major problem, however. His peers espoused his ideas but added excessive curlicues, doodads, and appendages to his box shape.

In England, Eastlake and his devotees tended to use oak or ash. Walnut was still the number-one wood in America, although it was waning in both popularity and availability. However, examples of Eastlake oak were manufactured in this country. His squarish lines remained in style from around 1870 until 1890.

Parlor table with Eastlake influence, as seen by the incised designs; 32" wide, 22" deep, 28" high. **$345**

Fall-front Eastlake parlor desk with incised lines and carving; 29" wide, 16" deep, 60" high. **$775**

Eastlake side chair with tufted velvet back, applied designs on uprights, and incised lines; 39" high. **$100**

Eastlake cane chair with incised designs and lines, set of 4. **$165** *each*

WILLIAM MORRIS

William Morris (1834–1896), an East-lake contemporary and one of the leaders of the Arts and Crafts Movement, was a designer who advocated a return to handcraftsmanship.

As a college student he had delved into church history. Therefore, it is fitting that he helped establish a company that specialized in ecclesiastical furnishings. Bookbinding, wood carving, embroidery work, tapestries, stained glass windows, murals, and mosaics were produced until his business expanded to serve secular interests as well. Wallpaper, furniture, and carpets received his attention.

To the average person Morris is probably more commonly associated with the Morris reclining chair. The seat and back cushions were loose in a plain wooden frame, and the back could be slanted by the movement of a metal rod.

Morris-type upholstered armchair with rolled arms and grotesques on leg uprights; 28" arm to arm, 39" high.
$375

JOHN RUSKIN

John Ruskin (1819–1900) and William Morris shared ideas. Ruskin, the London-born social reformer, writer, art critic and Oxford professor, helped promote the English Arts and Crafts Movement that spread to the United States.

Perhaps because the affluent Ruskin was acquainted with biblical teachings, he supported social reforms and spent much of his inheritance improving conditions of the working class. He established a model village, improved some tenements, and started educational institutions for workers.

Ruskin felt that good architecture was related to moral feelings and therefore was religious in tone. Authorities think Ruskin's and Morris's efforts and discussions did foster change.

ELBERT HUBBARD

Elbert Hubbard (1856–1915) worked for a time with his brother-in-law, John D. Larkin. The latter started a company under his name. By 1892 the Larkin Soap Manufacturing Company began in Buffalo, New York.

Hubbard was a writer, lecturer, and skilled advertising agent who helped develop the "Larkin Club." Women were encouraged to join to earn premiums in exchange for purchases. Free gifts for promoting Larkin clubs included "furniture, lamps, rugs, curtains, silverware, linens, and other lovely things for the home." Purchasers today look for the Larkin name on furniture. Some had mission lines but other styles were more prevalent.

While on a visit to England, Hubbard became impressed by ideas of the Arts and Crafts Movement. He came to accept William Morris's rejection of shoddy machine work.

Hubbard left the Larkin Company to establish a colony for artisans. As with Morris, bookbinding was his first interest. By 1895, handicraft artisans who joined Hubbard's East Aurora Colony in New York became known as "Roycrofters" and their products were generally marked "Roycroft." The symbol—the cross with an R in a circle and three dividing lines to represent faith, hope, and love—also appeared.

Roycroft original finish fall-front desk with name impressed on gallery; 43" wide, 19" deep, 58" high. $7,150 including buyer's premium

The Roycroft cross and orb symbol.

An example of a mark used by the Roycrofters.

The Roycrofters created pottery, leather articles, textiles, and metal objects, but they specialized in printing books. As buildings were added to the colony, furnishings were needed. Their straight-lined, handmade furniture would later be called the mission style, and first appeared in 1896. Their furniture was marked with their symbol and/or the name "Roycroft" in prominent places so it could be seen readily.

Mission Furniture

There are conflicting reports on how native-to-America mission furniture was conceived. Was it a derivative of the English Arts and Crafts Movement or did it have religious origins? Some say its roots are in the crude, straight-lined furnishings made by the unskilled Spanish monks and their converted Indian parishioners, who constructed utilitarian seats and tables for their rustic churches in the Old Southwest. This tale would both explain the name and the austerity of the mission style. However mission furniture was developed, Gustav Stickley most often is credited with making it popular and fashionable.

GUSTAV STICKLEY AND MISSION FURNITURE

Early in his life Gustav Stickley (1858–1942) worked as a furniture maker to learn about wood construction, styles, and merchandising. From the 1880s to the mid-1890s, Stickley and some of his brothers manufactured conventional furniture. The Stickley Brothers Company is mentioned in material obtained from the Grand Rapids, Michigan, public library. A leaflet entitled "Furniture—the Product of Pride" stated that from 1880 to 1900 more than eighty-five furniture manufacturers started businesses in that city, including the Stickley Brothers Company.

Gustav Stickley sought to improve the quality of furniture while reducing its cost. He and a partner opened a workshop in Eastwood, near Syracuse, New York, around 1895. In 1898, after returning from England, where he was influenced by the ideas of the Arts and Crafts Movement, he began experimenting with functional, solid, comfortable, durable, and rectangular-shaped furniture.

In 1900 he introduced his utilitarian wares at the Grand Rapids Furniture Exposition. His wood specialty was white oak, but he also used other indigenous varieties. Visitors realized that Gustav Stickley's Craftsman furniture had a new, uncluttered style. Other factories rushed to produce similar furniture.

Stickley continually experimented with finishes. Wood requires a coating of some type to help keep it from absorbing dirt or acquiring stains. For example, water that penetrates the wood leaves black spots. A sealing agent could help prevent this problem as well as help to accentuate the character and beauty of the wood.

Stickley liked fumed oak because it resembled patina, the natural darkening of furniture with age, use, and exposure to light and air. To obtain this appearance, Craftsman articles were moistened to open the pores and placed in an airtight compartment, where they were exposed to strong ammonia vapors for as long as forty-eight hours. After the furniture was hand-sanded, Stickley applied his own special coating to achieve one of three tones: a soft silver gray, a light brown, or a dark brown. Craftsman Wood Luster was rubbed on to complete the process.

Stickley cushions were covered with waterproofed genuine leather or sheepskin specially treated not to craze or check.

He believed in do-it-yourself projects and encouraged amateurs to send for his designs, leather, metal trim, instruction plans, and upholstery materials so that they could build quality furnishings inexpensively at home. Stickley felt that pleasing, well-designed, and well-executed furniture helped improve the moral fiber of a family.

The houses he designed varied in size to meet the neeeds of people at different economic levels. Stucco exteriors, oak beams, built-in cupboards, window seats, and bookcases were included.

Gustav Stickley sometimes used as many as three marks on a piece. His trademark was an old joiner's compass. Joiners depended on wooden pegs, wedges, or special joints such as mortises and tenons to unite the parts. Between the prongs of his patented joiner's compass, Stickley inserted the Dutch motto "Als ik kan" (as I can). Beneath this he placed his first and last name. The Craftsman label was another marking. By the time his 1913 catalog was published, Stickley modestly declared that most of his furniture "was so carefully designed and well-proportioned . . . that even with my advanced experience I cannot improve upon it."

Gustav Stickley went bankrupt in 1916, at about the same time his plain furniture went out of style. His words were prophetic, however, when he declared his furniture would be worth many times its original cost in fifty to one hundred years. Its durability and worthiness would make it so. Time proved him to be correct.

Rocker wirh corbels, pegs, new leather cushion, and replaced rockers with a red Gustav Stickley decal inside back stretcher; 25" arm to arm, 36" high. **$325**

Gustav Stickley's "Als ik kan" decal.

Gustav Stickley chair with slat back and rush seat; 36" high. **$1,500** *for set of 6*

CHARACTERISTICS OF QUALITY MISSION FURNITURE

1. Straight, sturdy, well-proportioned, and comfortable, with unadorned lines.

2. Mortise and tenon joints.

3. Through or exposed tenons.

4. A key, which is a small wedge-shaped piece of wood inserted through a slot in an exposed tenon, to add strength as well as decoration.

5. Pegs, pins, or plugs used to secure mortise and tenon joints.

6. A corbel, which is a bracket or brace that is fastened to the leg of an armchair directly beneath and attached to the arm as a support. It is used on tables and desks in a similar fashion.

7. Lightweight slender strips of wood, called muntins, that serve as dividers on the glass doors of a piece of furniture. They may run either vertically or horizontally.

8. Genuine leather or sheepskin cushions.

9. Handwrought heavy-gauge copper or iron hardware.

10. Extensive use of quarter-sawed oak.

11. Careful construction techniques, including properly fitted joints and well-constructed drawers and furniture backs.

OTHER MAKERS OF MISSION FURNITURE

Leopold and John George Stickley, who operated as L. and J. G. Stickley, were located at Fayetteville, New York. At first their plants were known as "The Onodaga Shops." Later they adopted a label that included a hand screw, the name "Handcraft," and "L. and J. G. Stickley." Another label, "The Work of L. and J. G. Stickley," also was used. Their brother, Gustav, felt they copied his Craftsman furniture, but the brothers were capable of producing well-designed furniture of their own. This company, Leopold and J. G. Stickley Company, remains in business today. Along with other lines, well-executed copies of the early mission styles brought out by Gustav and L. and J. G. Stickley are being produced.

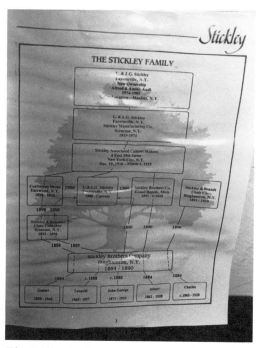

The Stickley family tree as seen in an L. and J. G. Stickley Co., Fayetteville, N. Y., catalog. This company is currently manufacturing the best examples of old mission furniture.

Sewing rocker with a metal label reading "Quaint Furniture, Stickley Bros., Grand Rapids, Mich."; 31" high. **$165**

Albert Stickley was president of Stickley Brothers Company. His mission line was labeled "'Quaint' Furniture, Stickley Bros., Co., Grand Rapids, Michigan."

Armchair in original finish with exposed arm tenons, corbels, pegs, and a paper label reading "Quaint Furniture, Stickley Bros."; 27" arm to arm, 40" high. **$295**

128

Limbert's Arts Crafts Furniture was made in Grand Rapids and Holland, Michigan. Their trademark showed a craftsman at a work bench surrounded by the words "Limberts Arts Crafts Furniture Made in Grand Rapids and Holland." In the manufacture of their mission-style furniture, much handwork was done on white oak, a wood used exclusively in their pieces. They also incorporated some of the styles found in early Dutch cabinetmaking.

Mission chair marked "Limbert" under left arm, with exposed arm tenons and pegs; 24" arm to arm, 39" high, set of 6. **$425** *each*

Library table that has a lift-up writing desk and inkwell when the drawer is fully opened. A manufacturer identification inside the drawer reads "Limbert Arts & Crafts Furniture Co."; 42" wide, 28" deep, 30" high. **$550**

The Shop of the Crafters, a little-known Arts and Crafts furniture manufacturer at Cincinnati, Ohio, produced a wide range of mission furniture and used the creed "Buy for simplicity, strength, and beauty; buy for permanency; and finally, make the home a consistent background for the life lived within." They produced an unusual and wide selection of cellarettes, floor and table lamps, shaving stands, cheval mirrors, and medicine cabinets.

Another little-known manufacturer of mission furniture was Lifetime Furniture of Grand Rapids. This company produced "Cloister Styles" which they advertised as the embodiment of simplicity, strength, and comfort. Both machine and hand craftsmanship were used in its construction.

Actually, all grades of mission furniture were marketed from about 1902 until 1916. Even the mail-order houses featured it. The 1908 Sears, Roebuck catalog announced *"Special Values in Mission Furniture."* It proclaimed that this style was not an experiment since it had retained its popularity after years of availability. It blended strength, comfort, beauty, and simplicity and received the approval of Arts and Crafts societies in both England and the United States.

Mission clock with brass pendulum and weights; 20" wide, 17" deep, 77" high. **$2,495**

Mission armchair with upholstered seat; 26" arm to arm, 37" high. **$150**

Mission rocker with upholstered seat; 27" arm to arm, 32" high. **$175**

Mission bench once used as a shoeshine stand in a barbershop; 62" arm to arm, 38" high. **$625**

Ecclesiastical bench with crosses in back splats and arm uprights; 46" arm to arm, 42" high. **$575**

Mission library table with a single drawer that opens in the front and back; 42" wide, 26" deep, 31" high. **$355**

Mission library table; 42" wide, 26" deep, 31" high. **$295**

Mission smoking stand; 12" wide, 11" deep, 30" high. **$165**

Mission fall-front desk with a label reading "Western Cabinet Co., Burlington, Ia."; 28" wide, 14" deep, 62" high. **$850**

CHAPTER 11
Accessories

Have you ever noticed the importance of accessories? Public places purchase antique items to add to their decor. Country-theme restaurants hang up hayforks, rustic rakes, and hand tools. A leading clothing store uses old-time cabinets and tables to display their wares.

Some items are acquired from country stores that were once like a crossroads department store. They used to sell everything: from coffee, tea, flour, sugar, crackers, vegetables and fruits to shoes, yard goods, thread, and garments.

Salesmen who called gave the shopkeepers useful display items that promoted their company's products. For example, thread was placed in various spool cabinets, ranging from a counter desk to a round or oval unit that rotated. These are used by housewives today. The desks can sit on top of an old sewing machine base. Spool cabinets of all sorts became end tables. Some versions serve as jewelry cases or hold collections of small items.

Refugees from other places are accepted as well. Barber, type, and dental cabinets have been adopted. A tavern table serves in a recreation area or kitchen. The old oak wall telephone may have a working modern telephone inside, contain a radio, or hold spices. Old frames and clocks have experienced a revival. Pleasing decor can be achieved through the display of unusual accessory items retrieved from the past.

Singer sewing machine that has been electrified and currently is in use; 36" wide, 17" deep, 31" high. **$115**

Sewing cabinet with applied molding, decorations, and a lift lid to pull up the machine head; 24" wide, 22" deep, 34" high. **$350**

Singer sewing machine; 36" wide, 18" deep. **$115**

Spool cabinet counter desk supplied by J. & P. Coats to storekeepers as an advertising promotion. Store accounts were kept inside the lift-lid section; 30" wide, 21" deep, 12" high. **$425**

Sewing machine with beading and pressed designs made by Wheeler & Wilson Mfg. Co., Bridgeport, Conn., patented March 25, 1890; 33" wide, 16" deep. **$125**

Richardson's spool cabinet with ten glass-front drawers and one made of wood; 20" square, 25" high. **$525**

Merrick's spool cabinet with a brass date plaque marked "July 20, 1897." Spools of thread were inserted through a covered hole in the top into the circular spool holder and when the holder was rotated by the knob at the top, the appropriate spool could be positioned for removal through the base door; 18" diameter, 20" high. **$700**

Label found on the back of the Richardson's spool cabinet.

J. & P. Coats spool cabinet counter desk resting on a metal sewing machine stand to form a self-standing desk; 30" wide, 21" deep, 12" high. **$425**

Label found on the back of the counter desk.

Barber cabinet with two drawers, a fall-front door, and open storage space in the base; 24" wide, 14" deep, 36" high. **$475**

Railroad desk with a slanted lift-lid top; 34" wide, 24" deep, 50" high at back, 46" high at front. **$425**

Type cabinet manufactured by the Hamilton Mfg. Co., Two Rivers, Wis., with all handles stamped "Hamilton Mfg. Co."; 37" wide, 22" deep, 43" high. $775

Barber cabinet with two swing-out doors and a fall-front door at the base; 16" wide, 9" deep, 19" high. **$195**

Corticelli Silk and Twist spool cabinet with 26 glass-front drawers and 4 wooden drawers; 45" wide, 18" deep, 43" high. **$1,350**

Dental cabinet; 26" wide, 17" deep, 59" high. **$975**

Type cabinet manufactured by Hamilton Mfg. Co., Two Rivers, Wis., Los Angeles, Calif., and Rahway, N. J.; 42" wide, 26" deep, 44" high. **$450**

Ansonia mantel clock; 14" wide, 5" deep, 22" high, **$250.** Clock shelf; 25" wide, 8" deep, 10" high. **$125**

Eight-day wall clock marked "Eclipse" (the model name) on back; 14" wide, 4" deep, 29" high. **$275**

Label on the back of the Ansonia wall clock (page 140) showing its prize medal award at the Paris Exposition in 1878.

Seth Thomas eight-day mantel clock; 15" wide, 5" deep, 23" high. **$250**

Ansonia wall clock; 14" wide, 5" deep, 38" high. **$800**

Machinist's chest with a label reading "Union, the Chest Co., Inc., Rochester, N. Y.," currently used to store jewelry, scarves, belts, and sundries; 20" wide, 8" deep, 13" high. **$175**

Waterbury regulator calendar wall clock; 16" wide, 5" deep, 34" high. **$425**

Frame with a decorative gold trim outline around picture and on the outer edge; 17" wide, 20" high. **$125**

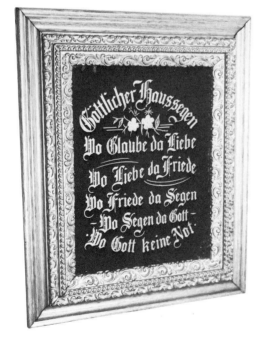

Frame with gold-leaf liner surrounding German religious motto, which has been translated in the space near the frame; 18" wide, 21" high. **$125**

Godly House Blessings
Where there is faith, there is love
Where there is love, there is peace
And where there is peace, there is blessing
Where there is blessing, there is God
And where God is—there is no need.

This label found on an oak wardrobe advertises Shallene Bros., dealers in furniture in Moline, Ill. Saving labels can preserve valuable historical and geographical information about the furniture you find.

141

Multilinear frame; 28" wide, 32" high. **$125**

Mirror with gold-leaf liner and oak outer surround, 27" wide, 30" deep. **$125**

Double-framed mirror, 29" wide, 51" high. **$150**

Framed mirror, manufactured by Life Time Furniture, Grand Rapids, Bookcase & Chair Co., Hastings, Michigan; 18" wide, 32" high. **$175**

Wall telephone made by Eureka Electric Co., Chicago; 12" wide, 32" high. **$345**

Wall telephone made by Stromberg Carlson; 9" wide, 6" deep, 18" high. **$310**

Tavern table with four compartments to hold beverages so the top surface remains free for card playing; 40" wide, 30" deep, 31" high. **$575**

Wall telephone made by Kellogg, Chicago, and patented Nov. 26, 1901; 11" wide, 6" deep, 23" high. **$250**

Glossary

Applied carving an ornament crafted separately and added to a piece of furniture

Apron the connecting piece on chairs, cabinets, and tables (see Skirt).

Artificial grain paint or stain applied to imitate the grain of a specific wood.

Bail handle a metal half-loop drawer pull attached to a backplate.

Beading a decorative trim that resembles a row of beads.

Buffet (sideboard) a piece of furniture for storing silverware, dishes, linens, or other tableware in a dining area.

Bulbous bulb-shaped. This term frequently is used to describe a plump, highly carved leg.

Cabriole leg a leg with a double curve flowing out at the knee, in at the ankle, then slightly outward again.

Chamfer a corner or edge cut off to form a slanting surface.

Cheval mirror a swinging looking glass supported by an upright frame. A cheval dresser has a large mirror of this type, usually set to one side of the hat cabinet.

Chiffonier a tall, narrow chest of drawers.

Chifforobe an article of furniture made with a chest of drawers on one side and a narrow wardrobe on the other.

Chip carving simple carved decoration made with a chisel or gouge.

Circa an approximate date. Most of the furniture in this book was made circa 1900.

Claw feet furniture feet that resemble an animal's paws.

Commode enclosed cupboard-type washstand.

Concave a surface that curves inward.

Convex a surface that curves outward.

Cornice top, horizontal molding on furniture.

Crest a carved piece on the top rail of a sofa or chair.

Cylinder a curved sliding top on a desk or secretary. Also, a desk or secretary that has a rounded front.

Divan a couch or sofa.

Drop lid or front a hinged lid on a desk that drops down to form a writing surface.

Eclectic adapting and combining designs and styles of various periods.

Extension table a table top that pulls apart so leaves may be added to enlarge it.

Fall-front a hinged lid on a desk that drops down to form a writing surface.

Finger hold a cutout part in a chair's back rail.

Fretwork an ornamental border perforated or cut in low relief.

Gargoyle originally a grotesquely carved ornamental creature projecting from a building; such a carving on furniture.

Grotesques figures or parts of figures of animals and people often mixed with flowers, fruits or foliage in an unnatural way.

Hardware metal used on a piece, including nails, screws, hinges, and the like. Pulls and handles are called hardware even when they are made of glass, ceramic, or other material.

Highboy a word in current use for a chiffonier.

Hoosier generic name for a kitchen cabinet with a pullout work surface, meal or flour bins, drawers, sifters, cupboard space, etc. This one-unit cabinet was made in the late 1800s and early 1900s in the Hoosier state (Indiana) and elsewhere. Different companies used other names for the cupboard.

Incised a design cut into the surface.

Marriage pieces of furniture combined as one when they were not originally a single unit. An example would be a bookcase top added to a drop-front desk to form a secretary.

Mortise and tenon the mortise is a slot or hole in a piece of wood. A tenon is a protruding tongue or prong in another piece of wood that fits snugly into the mortise to form a tight joint. They may be pegged where they join.

Muntins narrow dividing bars between window panes or glass on furniture such as a bookcase that can run vertically or horizontally.

Paw feet furniture feet that resemble animals' paws.

Pier glass or mirror a tall, narrow mirror often hung between two long windows.

Plain sawed boards cut lengthwise from the whole log in parallel slices that result in a pattern of stripes and elliptical Vs in oak.

Pressed back a design pressed into the back of a chair with a metal die to imitate carving.

Projection front a top drawer or section that overhangs the base.

Quarter sawed boards sliced from logs that have been cut in quarters lengthwise to expose large pith rays in oak.

Rolltop a flexible hood that slides down as a rounded lid on a desk.

Rung a crosspiece that connects cabinet, chair, or table legs at the bottom (also called stretcher or runner).

Scalloped a series of curves in an ornamental edge patterned after the shape of a shell.

Serpentine a snakelike curve on the fronts of furniture.

Shakers a religious community that constructed and sold plain, attractive, strong furniture to the public.

Sideboard see Buffet.

Skirt the connecting piece on chairs, cabinets, and tables. In chairs, it is beneath the seat; on tables, underneath the top; on cupboards and chests, at the bottom between the feet. It can hide construction details or add support (and also is called an apron).

Slant front the hinged drop lid on a desk or secretary that provides a writing surface when opened.

Slat horizontal crossbar in chair backs.

Splat the center upright in a chair back.

Splay slant out, especially chair legs that slant from the seat to the floor.

Stile the vertical piece in a frame or panel of furniture.

Stretcher see Rung.

Taborette (tabourette) a small plant stand.

Tambour a door made of wooden slats glued on a duck or canvas backing that operates either vertically or horizontally in a groove.

Turning shaping wood with chisels on a lathe to form table and chair legs or other items.

Veneer a thin layer of decorative wood glued over the surface of a cheaper wood.

Wardrobe a piece of furniture in which garments were hung before closets were common.

Bibliography

Books

Aronson, Joseph. *Encyclopedia of Furniture*. New York: Crown Publishers, Inc., 1965.

Ayars, Marcy, and Walter Ayars. *Larkin Oak*. Summerdale: Echo Publishing, 1984.

Cathers, David M. *Furniture of the American Arts and Crafts Movement: Stickley and Roycroft Mission Oak*. New York: New American Library, 1981.

Cole, Ann Kilborn. *How to Collect the New Antiques*. New York: David McKay Company, Inc., 1966.

Durant, Mary. *The American Heritage Guide to Antiques*. American Heritage Publishing Co., Inc., 1970.

Grotz, George. *The New Antiques*. Garden City, N. Y.: Doubleday & Company, Inc., 1964.

Hamilton, Charles F. *Roycroft Collectibles*. London: The Tantivy Press, 1980.

Mackay, James. *Turn-of-the Century Antiques*. New York: E. P. Dutton & Co., Inc., 1974.

Stickley, Gustav, and L. and J. G. Stickley. Stickley Craftsman Furniture Catalogs: *Craftsman Furniture Made by Gustav Stickley* and *The Work of L. & J. G. Stickley*. Introduction by David Cathers. New York: Dover Publications, Inc., 1979.

Swedberg, Robert W., and Harriett Swedberg. *American Oak Furniture Styles and Prices, Book II*, second ed. Radnor, Pa.: Wallace-Homestead Book Co., 1991.

———. *American Oak Furniture Styles and Prices, Book III*, second ed. Radnor, Pa.: Wallace-Homestead Book Co., 1988.

Catalogs

Chittenden & Eastman Company Furniture Distributors. *Catalogs*. Burlington, Iowa: Chittenden & Eastman Company, 1892 through 1950.

Israel, Fred L., ed. *1897 Sears, Roebuck Catalog*. New York: Chelsea House Publishers, 1976.

Life-Time Furniture, The Cloister Styles. Reprinted from original catalog. New York: Turn of the Century Editions, 1981.

Limbert Furniture. Reprinted from original catalog. New York: Turn of the Century Editions, 1981.

Montgomery Ward & Co., Catalog No. 99. Chicago, fall and winter 1923–1924.

Montgomery Ward & Co., Catalog No. 110. Chicago, spring and summer 1929.

Sears, Roebuck and Co. Catalog No. 154. Chicago, spring and summer 1927.

Schroeder, Joseph J., Jr., ed. *1908 Sears, Roebuck Catalog*. Chicago: The Sun Digest Company, 1969.

Shop of the Crafters at Cincinnati Furniture Catalog. New York: Turn of the Century Editions, 1983.

Periodicals

Koehler, Arthur. *The Identification of Furniture Woods, Circular No. 66*. Washington: United States Department of Agriculture, November 1926.

Index

About the Authors

When Bob and Harriett Swedberg research and write books, they travel thousands of miles. They meet many fine people who share their interest in preserving heritage articles for future generations. While they enjoy visiting museums, they do not include museum pieces in their books. The Swedbergs photograph only articles that are actually available to the public to purchase or are in the possession of people who have secured them to preserve and collect. To date, this couple has written books on oak, country furniture, wicker, Victorian, and advertising, as well as on refinishing and repairing antiques. They are available as speakers and enjoy teaching about America's heritage through antiques classes.